D0762352

Culinary Design and Decoration

Culinary Design and Decoration

William Emery
PhD, FRSA, FHCIMA

Illustrations **by**
Joyce Tuhill

A CBI Book
Published by Van Nostrand Reinhold Company

A CBI Book
(CBI is an imprint of Van Nostrand Reinhold Company Inc.)
Copyright © 1980 by Northwood Publications Ltd.

Library of Congress Catalog Card Number
ISBN 0-8436-2187-7

Printed in the United States of America

Published by Van Nostrand Reinhold Company Inc.
135 West 50th Street
New York, New York 10020

Van Nostrand Reinhold Company Limited
Molly Millars Lane
Wokingham, Berkshire RG11 2PY, England

Van Nostrand Reinhold
480 La Trobe Street
Melbourne, Victoria 3000, Australia

Macmillan of Canada
Division of Gage Publishing Limited
164 Commander Boulevard
Agincourt, Ontario M1S 3C7, Canada

16 15 14 13 12 11 10 9 8 7 6 5 4 3 2

Library of Congress Cataloging in Publication Data

Contents

Colourful Food – the art of design and decoration   7

1   The Principles of Culinary Design   9

2   Tools of the Trade   29

3   Decorative Materials   39

4   Appetisers – Hors-d'oeuvre, Salads and Soups   61

5   Sandwiches and Canapés   87

6   Fish, Meat and Poultry   101

7   Decorative Desserts   115

Index   131

Colourful Food
the art of design and decoration

Have you noticed how a clever woman can add a different accessory to last year's dress and the style becomes new, fresh and different? The type of imagination that transforms the ordinary into the exciting has its counterpart in many forms of artistic expression, not the least in the field of culinary arts.

So much time and trouble is spent in the preparation of food that it seems logical it should be presented with all the skill at the cook's command, for there is something stimulating about even the simplest meal if it is pleasing to the eye. However, making food attractive is one of the activities and skills that frequently puzzles the student cook, and sometimes the more experienced caterer. Often they do not know where to start, and even more often they do not know when to stop. Yet tasteful and imaginative decoration becomes quite simple once a rudimentary knowledge of design is understood, and it is realised that the materials being used impose certain limits on the artistic work that can successfully be accomplished.

Good decoration and presentation does not mean over-elaboration. It does not mean dressing up a pudding to look like a hedgehog (except perhaps at a children's party) or moulding a pâté into the shape of a pig. What it *does* mean, in a very simple form, is setting the food on a dish as neatly as possible and giving it colour and shape contrast in the form of a suitable garnish. Alternatively, it means decorating the food item in an appropriate manner bearing in mind the correct use of design elements and the impression that is to be achieved.

When considering decoration in any form, the best single standard is *restraint*. Food that gives the impression of over-decoration is distasteful to most people – therefore even for the most festive occasion, decoration and ornament should be used with discretion. Just as the jeweller displays one or two perfect gems in a setting to get maximum attention, so too should food be decorated for immediate 'eye appeal'. Too many items on a plate distract from the main one; too much garnish distracts from the food itself.

The word 'garnish' means to decorate or adorn. Yet, if the basic ingredients of a dish are not properly prepared, no decoration or adornment can make the food appealing. Food carefully prepared and carefully planned is beautiful in itself, and the garnish or decoration is used only to emphasise its inherent beauty.

There is much to be learned from the old-fashioned greengrocer in the way he presented his merchandise. The finest example of his produce was always on top of the pile. One fine mushroom served on a grill is more appealing than many pieces cut up and served on the plate; one or two perfect strawberries on top of the fruit salad are more attractive than several pieces mixed in with the other ingredients. So if you have one item that is especially fine, take full advantage of its basic appeal by placing it where the eye cannot miss it.

It is usually true that not all the ingredients in a dish can be perfect, but a little sorting and planning will always produce a few that are worthy of presentation. Three or four chunky strips of julienne chicken on top of the salad will hide many small bits and pieces. One or two whole prawns will make your customers think the salad is full of them, and they will eat with a better appetite.

There are, of course, many easy ways to create interest in the food you prepare and one of the most enjoyable is the contrasts produced by the simple combinations of natural materials. For example, chopped pimento mixed with potato salad, or a rosette of cream cheese nestling in a young, green lettuce leaf makes a colour contrast that would be enjoyed by most people. However, if the cheese were tinted with an artificial green colouring, most customers would think the result forced and unattractive.

There are a number of pitfalls into which the unwary cook can fall with regard to design, decoration and garnishing, and therefore, if one wishes to understand the elements of culinary design, a few rules must be remembered. In the first chapter these rules are explained.

Thereafter, the book is concerned with ideas and suggestions for decorating the most usual types of food served on a buffet, and illustrates how interesting colours, shapes and patterns may be used, and how design motifs can be made easily from commonplace materials.

This book has been written to encourage the reader to attempt new forms of presentation (when time and cost allow) and contains an assortment of ideas that over the years I have used or adapted, admired or invented in an effort to delight the eye and titillate the palate.

1

The Principles of
Culinary Design

The basic principles of design remain constant no matter to which art or craft they apply. The same design rules are followed by the successful architect or landscape painter, the chef or the confectioner. The scope of design, either simple or complicated, is restricted only by the limitation and flexibility of the materials. Thus the painter with a wider colour availability, can achieve more subtle effects than the chef *garde-manger* decorating a ham or galantine. But the same basic principles apply.

First of all, let us start with a definition of design. What is design? In simple terms, design is the *plan* which decides where and how to decorate a surface, and the placing of the decorative items in relation to each other. Good design is achieved when each design element used combines to produce a satisfactory completeness in relation to the whole.

A true explanation of the feelings aroused by good design can be likened to a similar feeling one has when hearing music. Just as the notes of music are extended in time, so design is extended in space. The various notes with their various time beats must be composed with a rhythmic structure if they are to be pleasing to the ear. Similarly the structure of the design elements must have a co-ordination and optical rhythm if they are to appeal to the eye and give effectiveness to the whole. These 'optical rhythms' may exist between lines, masses, forms and colours.

So the problem we face in our profession when constructing any design is in the formation of a pleasing and acceptable harmony of line, mass and colour in relation to the item we are going to decorate.

From the designer's point of view, line and mass often go hand in hand. To illustrate this relationship, we take a simile from the human body. Line is the skeleton; mass is the flesh. Line gives the impression, mass provides the form. Consequently correct line and mass arrangements are the very essence of good design, and correctly applied will produce the required qualities of rhythm, proportion, balance, harmony and so on.

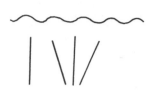

Fig. 1 to Fig. 6

Line

As we see, line is the skeleton of a design, and by its shape, contour and strength gives clear impressions of growth, purpose, calmness, repose and so on. In fact most people have come to associate certain lines, depending on how they are drawn, with definite qualities; and there is a remarkable agreement in the minds of most people regarding these impressions.

Small waves make the movement of a line go more quickly (Fig. 1).

Vertical lines and variations of vertical lines suggest dignity, repose, stability (Fig. 2).

The long, slow curve suggests calmness, luxury (Fig. 3).

Long, single curves suggest grace, beauty (Fig. 4).

Short curves suggest liveliness (Fig. 5).

Weak outlines lack direction and credibility and suggest decay and age.

In nature and in other objects we see examples of the power of line to tell a story. The spirals of a conch shell (Fig. 7) strongly suggest movement and growth; the radiating lines of a scallop shell (Fig. 8) give a clear impression of life and stability. Each line is necessary to the structure. All are different, but each is essential, and varies only in degree of curve or direction.

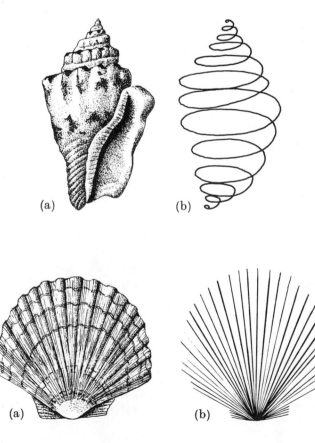

(a) (b)

Harmonious composition of line:
Fig. 7(a): Conch shell,
(b): structural detail
Fig. 8(a): Scallop shell,
(b): detail

(a) (b)

Fig. 9: Expression and
movement by line

Line will also produce very clear impressions of action or rest and repose
when used in the freehand piping of simple 'matchstick' men (Fig. 9).

Not only is harmony and rhythm of line necessary when using action
figures, but must be considered in any group of lines which are associated
with the 'total design'. As an example, let us take the border pattern.
We know that simple, flowing curves can produce an 'onward' movement
taking the eye round the perimeter (Fig. 10).

Fig. 10: Border pattern
with 'gentle' onward movement

As we see how different lines can give different impressions, and how a
border pattern with 'onward' movement is created, we can understand how
an opposite effect may be produced. By using variations of vertical lines,
as shown in Fig. 11, it is possible to create a 'restful' border design with
the central vertical motif as the inceptive axis and the smaller motifs as
the lines.

Fig. 11: Vertical lines
in a border

However, one of the requirements of the border pattern is that it should
be repetitive; border designs should be firstly composed of one or more
design units, and these should be used exclusively around the border. By
this means we convey the necessary feeling of unity in the total pattern.
The expression of the character and feeling of the border will depend upon
the style of the individual design unit. The two previous illustrations
show this quite clearly. However, should the border pattern be composed
of more than one *type* of unit (as is the vertical line pattern, Fig. 11) then
unifying 'links' must be used to carry from one design unit to the next,
and these 'links' must follow the same pattern as the design unit. If they
do not, the total pattern becomes disorganised. Notice that in Fig. 11
the link motif does follow the pattern of the main theme.

Now suppose we had used a 'scroll' link to join the individual units;

Fig. 12: Border with in-appropriate 'link'

you can see from Fig. 12 what an unhappy result we have. So a 'correspondence of line' must feature in the design.

Simple lines in a flowing curve can produce a pleasing effect, but when they are supported by secondary lines, then the onward movement is considerably emphasised. The design takes on a further dimension and a greater strength.

In Fig. 13, notice the way that the supporting lines curve in relation to the main stem of the design. You will see that these declensions firstly follow the same curve as the main stem, and then progressively move away from the original direction at regular, even intervals.

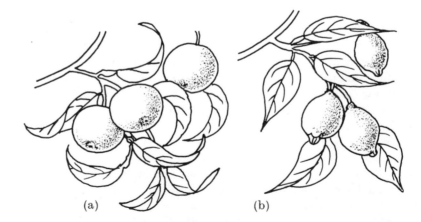

Fig. 13: Border with harmonious curves

Now just as we had 'correspondence of line', so we must have 'correspondence of contour' if the design is to have unity. This feature is particularly important when attempting to design a flower (or fruit) and leaf motif. Nature shows us many examples of just how harmony of line and contour is achieved. If we compare the *individual* shape of a leaf, for example, with the *total* shape of the tree from which it originates, we see a clear 'correspondence' between the two (Fig. 15); similarly with fruit and their leaves. Notice in the illustrations in Fig. 14 just how the contour of the leaves complements the contour of the fruit.

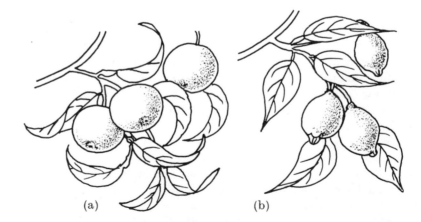

Correspondence of contour in fruit:
Fig. 15(a): Orange;
(b): lemon

(a)   (b)

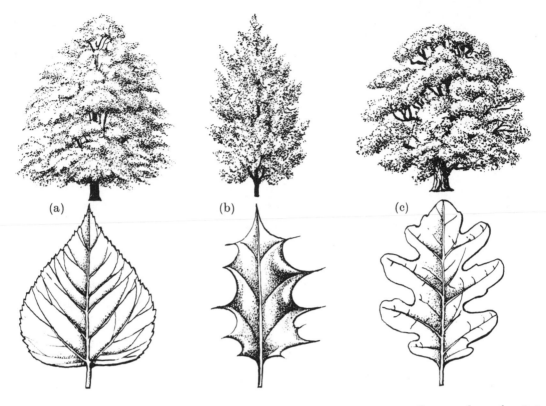

Correspondence of contour in trees:
Fig. 14(a) : lime;
(b) : holly;
(c) : oak

The Curve of Force

Nature also gives an excellent example of 'growth' line when she wants to support weight. If we examine the stems of flowers, we find that mostly the flower head is supported by a stem which has a particular type of curve. This individual line (Fig. 16) is known as the 'curve of force'. Because representational designs of flowers and leaves are so often used as decorative motifs in our profession, this line is one of the most important units to remember.

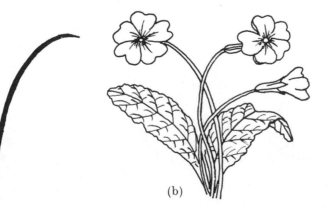

Fig. 16(a): The curve of force;
(b): nature's supporting curve

This curve is also used as a common design factor in the drawing of other natural shapes. Notice, in Fig. 17, how example (a) gives the clear impression of 'life and growth', while example (b) gives a contrary impression, of withering and decay.

Fig. 17(a): Growth;
(b): decay

Radiation

The principle of radiation is one of the most widely used elements in design, and is a term used to indicate the *direction* of a subsidary line from a main line or common centre (Figs. 18 and 19).

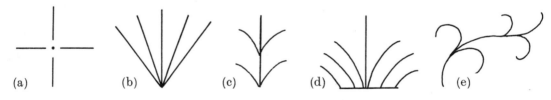

Fig. 18(a): From a centre;
(b): a point;
(c): an axis;
(d): a base;
(e): a curve

MASS

Mass (which includes shape and form) is used in conjunction with line to produce a fuller meaning to a design. Mass is the flesh that covers the skeleton (line) to give the whole greater weight. But to fulfil this purpose, mass must of course relate correctly with other features in the design.

Specific types of relationships will produce equally specific effects. To refer to the border pattern again, we have seen that ordered repetition with regard to a central point or axis gives rise to *symmetry*: relation-

Fig. 19: Examples of
radiation in nature

ships involving ordered movement result in *rhythm*. In addition, as we shall see, relationships of size give rise to *proportion*.

Symmetry

Symmetry is produced by reversing line or form with reference to a vertical axis. One example of this feature of design has been shown in the border pattern, Fig. 11. Other examples are shown in Fig. 20.

Fig. 20: Examples of symmetrical design

Rhythm

Rhythm in a design is obtained when the flow of movement has a definite and harmonious arrangement, as in Fig. 21.

Fig. 21: Examples of rhythm in design

Proportion

Proportion in a design refers to the relationship between areas, dimensions or parts. The early Greek philosphers formulated a theory of proportion in relation to the dimensions of a rectangle. They arrived at a conclusion that the 'ideal', that is to say the most pleasing proportion, was that in which the ratios between length and width were not easily recognisable. This principle resulted in the proportion known as 'the golden rectangle', (Fig. 22) whose short side was three-fifths of the long side. Indeed, so successful was this theory when put into practice that eventually the Parthenon was built entirely with stone cut to this dimension and proportion, and even today it is still regarded as one of the most beautiful buildings in the world.

It is equally interesting to note that among contemporary articles as diverse as windows and magazines, this proportion of width to length in a rectangular shape is the most popular. And in design it is an important proportion to remember, for it is useful when deciding shapes and sizes of many freehand cut-outs that may be required in representational designs.

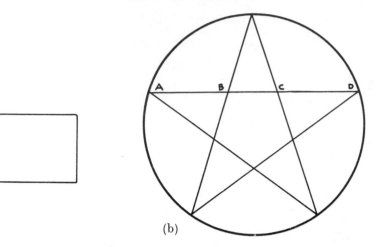

Fig. 22(a): The golden rectangle – the proportion; (b): a star design

The illustrations in Fig. 22 show the 3-unit to 5-unit proportion that is the base of the 'golden rectangle' theory, and also how this proportion is used to design an excellent 'star' shape within a circle. You will notice that the line AD is the total width of the star. The line AB is the ratio of 3 to 5. Thus if the line AD is drawn to 8 inches, the line AB (and of course CD) will be 3 inches. The ratio of AB to BC is 3 to 5 and the ratio of AC to AD is 5 to 8.

The 3-to-5 relationship is in fact just two proportion relationships which go to make up what is termed the *summation series,* used lavishly by nature to give beauty and proportion to many objects. The series which is 2 : 3 : 5 : 8 : 13 : 21 : 34 and so on is explained as follows – 5 being the *sum* of 2+3, and 8 being the *sum* of 3+5, thus we find that the sum total of two adjoining figures when taken as a proportion to the sum total of the *following* two figures, provides a ready-made mathematical formula for good proportion.

This summation series can be seen in many natural growths. If we count the leaf points on a pine cone, we find that the total counting around the bottom row will have a number that will fit into the summation series if taken in relation to the *next* row of leaf points. Similarly with the seed arrangement in, say, a sunflower. The outer ring of seeds will fit into the

Fig. 23: Proportions. (a): 2 to 2; (b): 3 to 5

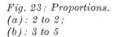
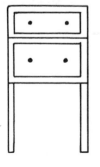
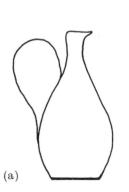
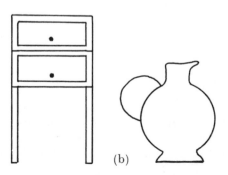

(a)

(b)

series if taken as a proportion of the next row of seeds. It is quite a remarkable feature.

So therefore, in order to get a pleasing proportion to our mass or form, we must adjust the size and *shape* to fit the 3-to-5 rule. In the examples in Fig. 23, notice the improvement in the design when we change the size relationship from a 2 to 2 (equal proportion) to a 3 to 5.

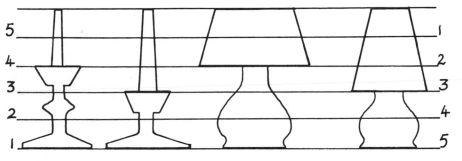

Fig. 24: Proportion divisions illustrating the 3-to-5 principle

In catering design and decoration, when we are concerned with the aspects of proportion in relation to flowers and leaves and similar features, we find that when the design factors are numerous then possibly the design will be overcrowded and adjustments may be difficult. It is as well to remember, therefore, that the best examples of good proportion are found when the components are neither too many nor so close in size that it is difficult to decide which is the dominant one. It is for this reason also that simplicity in design is recommended.

The following example, Fig. 25(a), shows bad proportion of a flower and leaf design. Notice that the central flower (which should be the the only

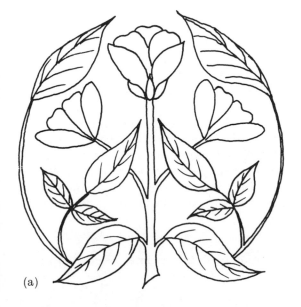

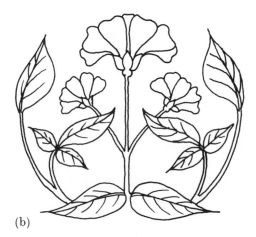

Fig. 25(a): bad proportion;
(b): better proportion

(a)

(b)

focal point or the dominant factor) is too small in relation to the leaves which support it on both sides, and also to the two subsidiary blooms; Fig. 25(b) gives a better proportion.

Unity

Unity is the harmonious relationship between all parts of the design; the ability to have this 'built-in' quality of holding together should be the constant test when judging any design in its initial stages. This relationship is dependent in the first place upon logical and ordered thought on the part of the designer, and then by the application of the idea to the type of material to be used to make the design.

The design must also be applicable to the form, and it will be readily understood that a design suitable for a square or oblong panel would not be suitable to a round panel or form. Consequently, although the main theme of the design may be similar, the specific treatment of each of the design elements will differ. This modification is necessary so that the design compliments the form.

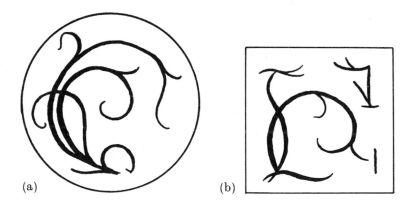

Fig. 26: A similar pattern for (a): a round, and (b): a square form

(a)   (b)

Variety

It is also necessary to introduce variety into a design. This is not difficult to do if these few rules are followed. Shapes of units or parts should vary. The declension of curves in a design should vary. The sizes of units should vary.

In the following examples, notice how the declension of the curves is varied, as are the sizes of the circles that go to form the design mass, Fig. 27(a). Notice a similar feeling and idea in Fig. 27(b). Here the three curves are different, one giving a strong contrast but being completely unified and part of the design. The individual curves, too, show variety and thus make them more interesting as examples of simple design units.

Balance

Balance is the optical co-ordination of all factors in a design, and exists

(a)　　　　　　　　　　　(b)

Fig. 27 : *Variety in line and form*

in mass, form, colour and, it should be remembered, in *area*. Balance calls for a real or imaginary line (inceptive axis) drawn vertically, horizontally or across the area and around which the design units will be placed.

Balance may be produced in the following ways:

1 Formal balance – whereby equal areas (or weights) of mass or line are placed on either side of a central axis. A variation of formal balance, termed *counter-balance,* is achieved when the inceptive axis runs across (diagonally) the area.
2 Informal balance – when units of mass may differ in size on each side of the axis, but when viewed together in the completed design produce equal optical balance.

Simple formal balance can most easily be achieved by placing the units of mass or line on equal sides of the base area upon which one is working. This is shown in the following example, Fig. 28.

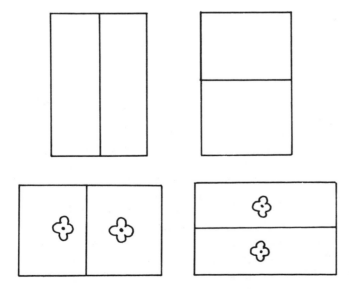

Fig. 28 : *Inceptive axis and formal balance of mass*

Counter-balance is achieved when the units of mass are similar in number and optical weight but are placed diagonally across the base, as in Fig. 29.

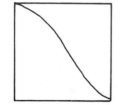

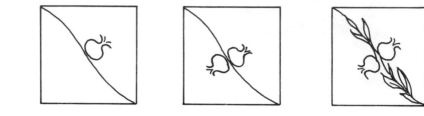

Fig. 29: Counter balance with a diagonal inceptive axis

Informal balance is obtained by using design elements that are not of equal optical weight or even of a similar type. Notice that in Fig. 30(a) the two smaller units are placed on one side of the panel to balance the one large unit on the other side. In Fig. 30(b) the single single unit of mass – the flower – is balanced by the heavy hanging leaves.

The design possibilities when using informal balance of line and mass are much wider and more effective than those produced by formal balance. Greater interest in design patterns can be maintained by the fact that neither the inceptive axis nor the elements of mass need to be centrally placed on either side of the design panel.

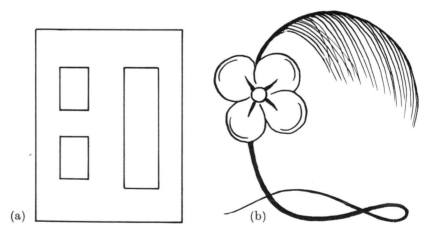

Fig. 30: Examples of informal balance

(a) (b)

DESIGNING OF SPECIAL SHAPES

The designing of different shapes presents problems in space division and in fitting the design to follow the form of the shape. Examples of this are shown on page 18, Fig. 26. These problems are not entirely relevant to catering design, but rather more in confectionery design and decoration. However, the principles offer an exercise in design formulation.

For example, when designing a vertical area, the movement of the design must have an upward tendency, but with sufficient stability at its base. The following example shows how this is done.

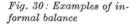

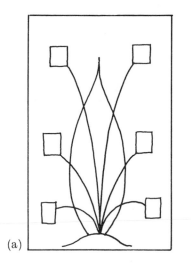
(a)

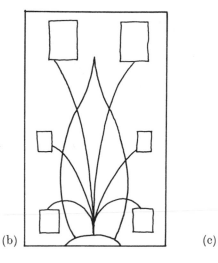
(b)

(c)

Fig. 31: Progressive design of a vertical panel

In Fig. 31(a) you will see the rough distribution of mass and line. There are three points of emphasis on each side of the inceptive axis, which is in this case the central leaf motif. This arrangement is quite without interest as a design. Fig. 31(b) shows how the masses have been rearranged, varied in size and consequently in proportion. This effect is more pleasing. The base has stability and the lines carry an upward movement to the focal point at the top of the design. The only wrong features are the two central points of mass, and the rather bad divisions of the areas of space. In the third illustration, Fig. 31(c), these displeasing elements have been removed by extending them into 'leaf forms' which result in the relation between line, mass and space.

As far as possible all vertical areas should be treated in a similar manner for both representational or abstract design.

The following examples show the treatment of verticals when using line only as a design element. Notice again that the base is sturdy and the lines upward and dynamic.

Fig. 32: Treatment of vertical panels

Both triangular and half-circular panels require the same approach: strong base, dynamic and upward line leading to a focal point. Notice in both examples how the total design fits the form or shape. In the *triangle,* Fig. 33(a), the very shape pulls the eye from the base upward to the point,

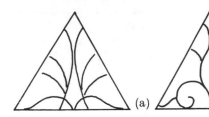

Fig. 33: Treatment of triangles and half-circles

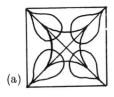

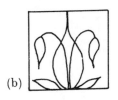

Fig. 34(a): Motif with radiation from centre; (b): the design which fits the shape

and the design follows that feature closely. With the *half-circles*, Fig. 33(b) a similar situation is evident, although the shape itself is not so dynamic or forceful. But still, the eye tends to start at the horizontal line base and be drawn towards the top of the shape. Again, the design follows the shape.

Square panels may be designed either with a focal point in the centre, as in Fig. 34(a), or may follow the shape of the square by altering a design to fit the shape, as in (b).

If you turn example (a) 45 degrees, it becomes a diamond shape, and the pattern and design are equally suitable. However, should an 'elongated' *diamond* shape be used, a slightly different approach is required. There are two alternatives, both of which work well. Either the design elements should be similar on either side of the imaginary inceptive axis, as shown in Fig. 35(a), or there can be one point of radiation from the lower end of the shape, as shown in Fig. 35(b). When either method of design is used the lines should be drawn with an upward tendency, with supporting lines towards the side angles.

Oval panels should have the inceptive axis from side to side both horizontally *and* vertically, with both sides of the design of similar weight and construction.

Fig. 35: Treatment of elongated diamond
Fig. 36: Treatment of oval panel

Circular panels should be treated in such a manner that their inherent 'static' form is emphasised. When designing with abstract motifs, special attention should be paid to radiation and stability. Straight lines, radiating from the centre and connecting the units of mass, give a feeling of repose. This treatment of a circular panel is the most common in culinary work and is used when designing decorative platters or large salad arrangements. When a flower and leaf design is called for, the 'roundness' of the circle is emphasised, as shown in Fig. 26(a), page 18. An alternative is to use what is more or less a border pattern, but bring it *into* the major area, as shown in Fig. 37.

We have now discussed the fundamental rules which must be followed when planning a design of any kind. The reader may now understand more clearly what was meant by the statement that there was an affinity between design and music. In music we have an octave of eight notes, but within this series are sharps and flats; each note may be of long or short duration; some notes may join with others to give harmony, while others played together produce discord. And so on throughout the whole keyboard. Similarly with design. The various factors must be used to create optical harmony. Badly used, they will produce optical discord – and a poor design. That is why it is so important to take time to think out any design before it is attempted. Sketch it out on paper; see if it sits happily within the framework of the area. If there *is* a discord, move the design pieces around until you get the correct effect. Soon, it becomes second nature to produce good design.

Fig. 37 : Circular pattern as design feature

THE MAIN TYPES OF DESIGN

Culinary design falls into two groups:

(1) Representational design (and design by *impression*);
(2) Abstract design.

Representational Design

Design falls into the first group when it is concerned with (or 'represents') an immediately recognisable form or shape, such as a butterfly or a leaf motif. To be successful the design must be so executed that it offers an immediate recognition, and shows quite clearly the characteristics of the shape or pattern.

Because of the limitations of our design materials – which must be edible – we do not have the range of colours, shading and versatility available to designers using a painter's palette. So whereas the very experienced artist/designer can produce decoration that is truly magnificent and, indeed, almost exactly 'true to life', in many cases our representational designs tend to be representational *impressions*.

In other words, modifications are most certainly acceptable in attempting the true-to-life concept (as Fig. 38 shows), although in many cases the execution is formal and stylised. The design is immediately recognisable as a flower and leaf because we have used correctly coloured materials to make the individual motifs – green leek for the leaves, red radish for the flowers and so on; thus the design has an acceptable degree of realism. In addition, of course, the individual shapes of the design units are arranged so that they suggest a flower and leaf design. This type of decoration is quite easy to execute, providing the student has an understanding of the principles of design.

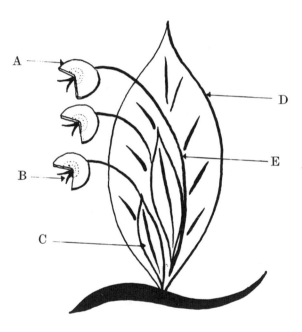

Fig. 38: Stylised representational design.
A = radish, B = sliced olive,
C and D = leek, E = chive.

There is another rather more advanced decorative technique which is extremely useful when cold buffet decoration is necessary. This is the 'unit' technique, based upon the principle that individual units when placed correctly can produce an acceptable 'whole' design. It is common to see this type of work on *chaudfroid*, when the units are very often black aspic cut-outs, but may be in other colours.

Notice how the two illustrations in Fig. 39 have been broken down into their fundamental shapes by the designer, and how emphasis has been given to both the outline and the essential internal structure; how some of the lines have been given extra strength, so that the whole shape will be immediately understood and acceptable. As you will see, this emphasis is obtained by using variations of curve declension, each curve being positioned with regard to its relative importance to the whole structure of the design.

(a)　　　　　　　　　　(b)

Fig. 39: Decoration by the 'unit' technique

There are one or two further points to be noted in these designs, which relate to the lessons we have learned in earlier pages. With the butterfly design, notice how the 'roundness' of the wings has been achieved by placing two heavy units at the top of the design, echoed by smaller units underneath which follow the main contour. The spread and the strength of the wings has been done by *reversing* the shape, so that emphasis is from the body towards the outer part of the design. Similarly with the under wings; these have been given quite heavy units so that the total shape of the design becomes enclosed and appears as a whole.

The leaf or tree, Fig. 39(b), is handled in a similar manner. The outline is strong; the inner lines, which spring from a horizontal line base, give the impression of upward growth, and of course the leaf and stem design at the base of the main feature finishes off the total impression.

There are two things that these designs have in common. That is the general *shape* of the design units. The long, flattened curve heavy at one end and light at the other is ideal for use in a design that needs to emphasise its 'roundness' or 'growth'. Both designs require this treatment. On the one hand, the butterfly shape is a variation of the round; the leaf (or tree) needs a fullness of shape to give it life, and the top part of the design, together with the internal pattern, gives it the necessary feeling of growth.

By contrast, notice how ineffective and optically unacceptable (unbelievable) are the same design motifs when all the lines are given the same weight or strength (Fig. 40).

So again we have demonstrated the essential fact that the individual

Fig. 40: Examples of weak design

shape unit must emphasise the form. This is in exactly the same way as the shape of the leaf emphasises the total outline of the tree, as we saw in Fig. 15 on page 13.

Compare this with the next illustrations. Here we have two tree shapes executed again with unit designs. But because the shape of the tree (as a total shape) requires a different emphasis, the shape of our units must be quite different also. Whereas the butterfly and leaf/tree designs required curved design units to bring out their essential shapes, the trees in the illustration below require small *triangular* shapes to bring out *their* character. (The branches are composed of chive, with finely-chopped parsley sprinkled over).

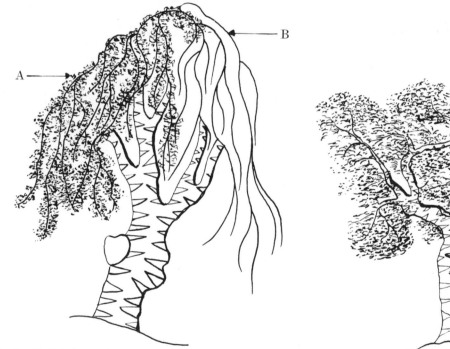

Fig. 41: Unit designs using triangular shapes.
A = chives, B = parsley

Abstract Design

Abstract design is most often used in the creation of a border pattern or as a basic design feature of salad bowls or platters of cold meat. This aspect of design is concerned with emotional or intuitive appeal. As we have discussed earlier, and as examples have shown, most people have come to associate lines, forms, mass and colour with definite qualities. These in turn evoke various subconscious feelings; thus curved lines give clear impressions of grace, charm and so on, and geometric form conveys feelings of sturdiness and solidity if associated with a square or triangular shape.

COLOUR

One cannot possibly leave the subject of design and decoration without mentioning the vital factor of colour. Possibly the simplest means of stimulating interest in culinary design is by contrasting different colours. Small areas of intense colour against a larger mass of a neutral colour can be very effective in highlighting the food as a whole.

In the decoration of platters or any sort, it is necessary to regard the colour scheme as an intrinsic part of the design from its inception. As we have seen, form and colour cannot be separated, for the effectiveness of a design may be ruined by ill-chosen colour contrasts.

The associative factor of colour is very strong, presumably because of constant visual impressions from childhood. In those early days we realised that the sky was blue, that cabbage was green and indeed that this was the natural order of things. Thus if we saw the sky as green and cabbage as blue in any decorative pattern, we would immediately reject it. We therefore have come to associate a certain green with spring, with freshness and coolness; white with snow, purity, cleanliness . . . and so on. Indeed, because this associative factor is so strong, it is hard to think of Christmas from a decoration point of view without associating it with the colours red, green and white.

In fact there are certain colour combinations which have become established as the 'colour trade marks' of special events. Here are a few examples:

New Year's day	White, apple green contrast
St. Valentine's day	White, deep red contrast
St. Patrick's day	White, emerald green contrast
First day of spring	Yellow, coral or apple green
Easter	Yellow and chocolate brown
April Fool's day	Pale yellow, green contrast
Mother's day	White, pink contrast
May day	Pastel shades contrasting
First day of summer	Pastels of spectrum – *not* blue
Hallowe'en	Orange and dark brown
First day of winter	White, dark green contrast
Christmas	White, red and green

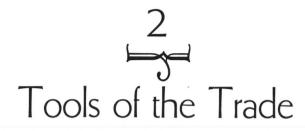

Tools of the Trade

The selection of knives, cutters and moulds for decorative work in the kitchen is an important prerequisite in the correct preparation of the items.

Basic Knives and their Uses
A wide range of kitchen knives in different shapes and lengths is available and each is suited to a certain cutting task. The following list is a basic requirement in the commercial kitchen:

Boning knife with a 6in (15cm) narrow blade;
French cooks' knife with an 8in (20cm) blade for heavier cutting;
Paring knife with a 3in (8cm) blade for vegetable peeling and cutting;
Garnishing knife with a $3\frac{1}{2}$in (9cm) partly serrated blade;
Carving knife – thin 9in (23cm) blade, plain/serrated for carving roast meat, poultry and ham;
Fruit knife with curved blade for grapefruit and other citrus fruits.

In addition, the possession of a pair of strong kitchen shears is recommended, for they are most useful for cutting lobster and poultry.

Over the years, great improvements have been made in the manufacture and design of kitchen knives. Today's knives are sharper; they hold their cutting edge longer and they are well balanced and easier to keep in good condition. The basic metal for knife blades is steel alloy with carbon added for strength. To this, chromium is often added, producing stainless steel. Blades of this metal are stainless throughout and they will never rust or spot. Vanadium alloy can also be added, further strengthening the blade. Carbon steel can be plated with chromium and this gives the advantages of stainless steel, until the plate wears off. The best blades are made of high carbon stainless steel with vanadium added. Next come high-carbon stainless steel, then high carbon steel with chromium plating and finally high carbon steel.

Knives are manufactured in three basic steps. 1, the shaping of the steel; 2, grinding the cutting edge, and 3, finishing the blade and fixing the

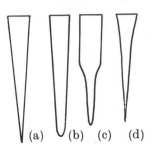

Fig. 42: The four types of grind. (a): Hollow; (b): roll; (c): flat; (d): concave

Fig. 43: 'Tang' extends the full length of the handle

handle. The blade is shaped by 'forging' – that is, hammering a bar of selected metal into a knife blade. Once shaped, the blade is heated in a furnace to a very high temperature, then quenched with cold water. This heating and quenching process is called 'tempering'. The first tempering leaves the metal too brittle so it is reheated, this time at a lower temperature, then quenched again. The quality of the heat treatment can be tested when you are buying a knife, by trying to bend the blade. If the blade bends and then snaps back into place, it has been properly tempered and has developed the necessary qualities of flexibility. Next, the cutting edge is ground on to the blade. The method determines both its sharpness and its durability.

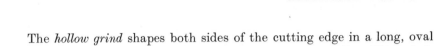

The *hollow grind* shapes both sides of the cutting edge in a long, oval curve. The blade is then sharply bevelled to the cutting edge. This grinding, also used on straight-edged razor blades, is expensive. However, the cutting edge stays sharp and requires only occasional resetting.

The *concave grind* sharpens both sides of the cutting edge into concave curves.

The *roll grind* is obtained by placing the lower part of the blade between two sharpening wheels that are rotating towards the blade. This method is inexpensive.

The *flat grind*, also called the 'V' or 'taper' grind, is a long, flat, even grind from top to bottom of the blade, with no curvatures.

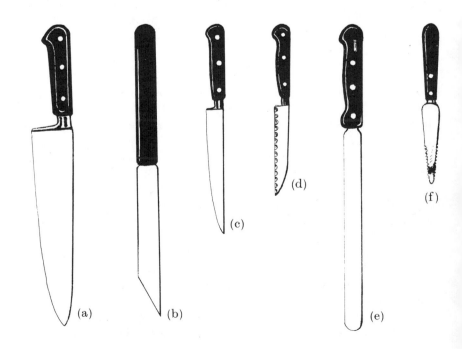

Fig. 44(a): French cooks' knife; (b): boning knife; (c): paring knife; (d): vegetable garnishing knife; (e): thin-blade carving knife; (f): citrus fruit knife

Knives may also have a scalloped, serrated or saw-toothed edge, all of which offer special advantages in different cutting jobs and hold their keenness indefinitely.

The handle of the knife should also be scrutinised for smoothness, durability and appearance. When a blade is forged the 'tang' – that is the extension to which the handle is attached – should be shaped also. For a knife to be durable and sturdy, the tang should extend at least one-third of the overall handle length in small knives, and for larger knives a full-tang construction is essential. This full tang construction provides extra strength and good balance and should be fastened to the handle by high-compression rivets.

Other Tools and Aids

Apart from knives, there are many tools and utensils needed if attractive patterns and designs are to be produced. Below is a list of requirements which you will find of considerable use and which will allow you to undertake a wide range of decorative effects.

Butter curler   A hooked tool which, when scraped along the surface of the butter pat, produces attractive curls.

Metal cutters   Both round and scalloped cutters are used for cutting pastry bread, croûtons and components to be used on large presentation items.

Cutters (aspic)   Both medium and small-sized fancy metal cutters are used for smaller decorative effects and to cut items to go on a *chaudfroid* base.

Egg slice   To cut hard-boiled eggs into neat slices.

Mandoline   Used for slicing vegetables such as cucumber very thinly and very quickly.

Moulds   Aluminium moulds of various shapes: hearts, houses, fish, bouquets of flowers and also moulds for savarins, jellies, etc.

Parisienne cutter   To produce melon balls or potato balls and to scoop the flesh from fruit and vegetables.

Piping bags (and tubes)   Essential for the production of savoury canapés and any piping work that is needed.

Patty pans   Various shapes from the conventional 'round' to boat-shaped and basket-shaped. Useful for both savoury and dessert production. Under this section we include 'cream horn' moulds.

Pastry brush   For putting aspic on any surface and brushing pastry with glaze or egg wash.

Spatula   To spread cream mixtures, butter, icing sugar, etc.

Tweezers   Necessary when placing small decorations on to a base and invaluable for dipping small decorations in aspic.

Vegetable scorers   To cut grooved designs and lines in fruit and vegetables.

Perhaps a little more should be said about aspic cutters. These cutters are found in any kitchen where decoration is given an important place in the merchandising scheme of things. They are usually made of tin in sets of twelve, and come in two sizes. The medium size is usually used for

*Fig. 45: Fancy aspic cutters
(medium size)*

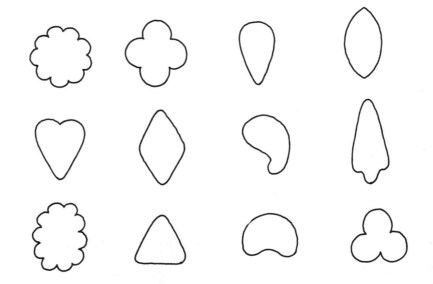

*Fig. 46: Small aspic cutters
(actual size)*

single cut garnishes, for example those to be placed on 'open' sandwiches. These cutters give simple but very attractive shapes and can therefore provide interesting contrasts in both colour and shape.

The smaller aspic cutters (Fig. 46) are used to produce designs and motifs that are components of a pattern rather than to give individual design effects, and a set should be regarded as indispensible. From the twelve assorted shapes a wide variety of flowers and border patterns may be produced, as the following illustrations will indicate. Stems and leaves from chive, spring onion tops, cucumber skin or leek leaves have been used in some cases to link a design or to give a clearer impression of the design idea.

Almost any edible garnish may be used with these cutters. For example, when making designs from No. 1 and No. 2 the flowers may perhaps be cut from the white of a hard-boiled egg, in which case you could sprinkle a little chopped yolk in the centre of each one. Alternatively, the flowers could be cut from red pimento, with perhaps a tiny piece of green olive in the centre.

There are two important points to remember when attempting this type of decoration. The first is to be sure that whatever materials you use – tomato, radish, olive and so on – the slices are *not too thick*, or the design will be heavy and clumsy. The second is that in all cases when you use chive or other green material as stems to support a flower motif, these stems *must* have a 'natural curve' (remember 'the curve of force' in Chapter 1 ?). In addition, the stems must not be too thick or too heavy for the type of flower they will support.

Fig. 47: Using No. 1
aspic cutter

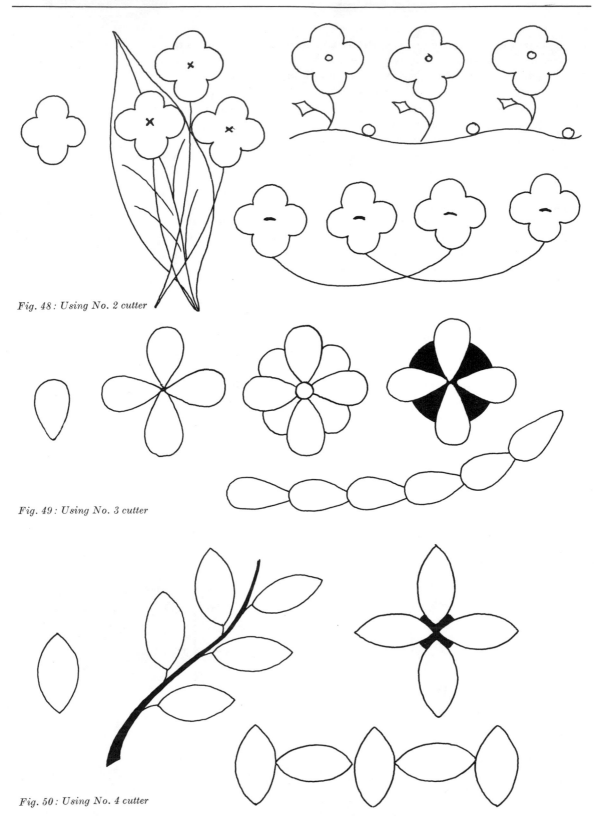

Fig. 48 : Using No. 2 cutter

Fig. 49 : Using No. 3 cutter

Fig. 50 : Using No. 4 cutter

Fig. 51: Using No. 5 cutter

Fig. 52: Using No. 6 cutter

Fig. 53: Using No. 7 cutter

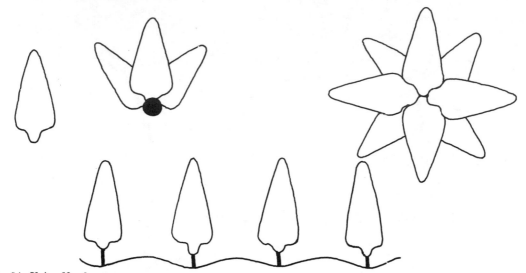

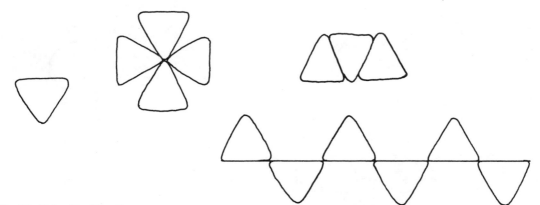

Fig. 54 : Using No. 8 cutter

Fig. 55 : Using No. 9 cutter

Fig. 56 : Using No. 10 cutter

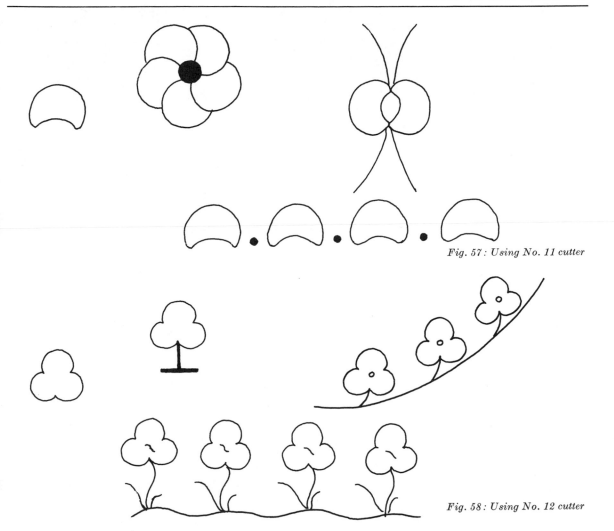

Fig. 57 : Using No. 11 cutter

Fig. 58 : Using No. 12 cutter

3

Decorative Materials

There are of course very many materials and foods that are used to make cut-outs and garnishes for the buffet table. In this chapter we show the more usual types and suggest how they may be used.

Anchovy

These tiny fillets of salt fish should first be wiped with a damp cloth to remove the oil, then smoothed down with the flat of a knife. They can then be cut into the required shapes. The most common manner to cut anchovy is diagonally, producing 'diamond' shapes which can then be used to make a star or leaf motif (Fig. 59), perhaps linked by chive stems.

Thin strips of anchovy are sometimes used to 'bind' a decoration, to represent string. For this the fillet is cut lengthwise in very thin strips. It is best to use a single-sided (Ever-Ready) razor-blade for this delicate work. In Fig. 60, we use the anchovy string to finish off a slice of hard-boiled egg garnished with an asparagus tip.

Another simple way to use anchovy as a garnish is to roll the fillet into a circle and just place it on the item you wish to garnish. A ring of sliced French bread spread with a little creamed chicken and a curled anchovy as garnish is delicious. Another very simple idea is to cut the anchovy fillet in half and wrap it around a stuffed olive, like a scarf. This present-

Fig. 59: Anchovy 'diamonds'
Fig. 60: Anchovy fillets used as 'string'

ation is excellent with a veal dish or to add a touch of strong flavour when needed.

Artichoke

The globe artichoke is a thistle-type vegetable comprising a base (the 'fond') which has a slightly conical hairy centre (usually called the 'choke') and overlapping leaves which cover the base. The 'fond' is the most important part of the vegetable, and the one used extensively in good-class cuisine.

One of the easiest methods of preparing the fonds is to put the whole artichokes into a cold water and vinegar solution and cook them until nearly tender – about 15 minutes after the liquor comes to the boil. Allow the artichokes to cool, take off the outer leaves to the bottom of the vegetable, and the fond with the choke will be exposed. With a sharp knife, trim the base so that it will sit well; then, with the back of a small spoon, carefully scoop out the choke, taking care not to break the edges of the saucer-like fond. Now you may drop the cleaned fonds into another vinegar and water solution and finish the cooking process when required.

Fonds d'artichauts farcis are often used as a garnish or as a buffet item. The scooped-out heart is filled with a savoury mixture and garnished with, for example, sliced stuffed olives.

Fig. 61: Artichoke fond (or heart) and choke

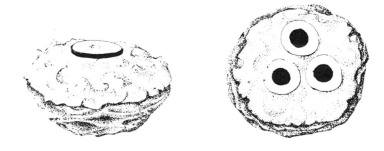

Fig. 62: Stuffed artichoke hearts

Asparagus

Canned asparagus is normally used for all cold buffet decoration or sandwich filling. There are two main types used – the spears and the tips. The latter are the smaller, being about 2in (5cm) long, while the spears measure about 5in (13cm). The tiny tips are preferred for all delicate work, but the larger spears can be cut or split in half if necessary.

Small bunches of asparagus are often used as a garnish for *gros pièces*, such as a standing rib-roast or a whole ham. One method of presentation is to stack asparagus tips in bundles of three and 'bind' them with a strip of red pimento. They are then arranged at intervals around the display platter (Fig. 63(a)).

If you are serving asparagus as a course on the buffet, an attractive method of presentation is shown in illustration (b), and of course this lattice design may equally well be used to garnish a large platter.

Opposite: Salmon trout with caviar (See page 43)
Overleaf: Avocado, decorated and in salads (See page 67)

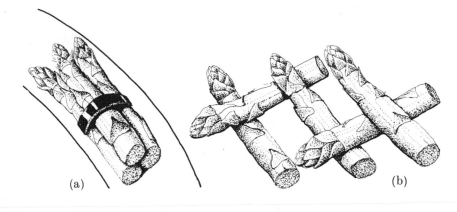

(a)
(b)
(c)

Fig. 63: Asparagus used as (a): stacks; (b): lattice; (c): upright bundle

Another simple idea (Fig. 63(c) is to use asparagus tips as garnish by arranging the tips level, then cutting the stalks to stand evenly. Place a bundle of four or five upright and ring them with a band of raw onion or red or green pepper.

Beetroot

Cooked beetroot is not often used as a decorative material because it has a great tendency to stain anything with which it comes into contact. However, there are a few occasions when this vegetable can be used, and the most popular manner is to cut it in the form of a flower. For this purpose, it is necessary to choose very small cooked beets. With an apple corer cut out the centre of the beet, taking great care not to cut right through to the base, Fig. 64. This centre piece may be extracted by cutting it away with a small knife. Decide how many 'petals' you wish your flower to have, then form them by cutting from the top downwards into the required number of sections, (b); again, do not separate at the root end. Open the petals carefully with the point of a knife, (c).

(a)
(b)
(c)

Fig. 64: Stages in cutting a beetroot flower

Broccoli

Tiny bunches of blanched broccoli are most useful as decorative material, as an individual garnish, as part of a border pattern or as a 'foliage' base for a larger floral motif (Fig. 65).

In Fig. 66 a small branch of broccoli is used as a garnish for a glazed tartlette filled with a savoury mixture. Naturally, when used in this

Fig. 65: Broccoli florets as base

A Previous Page: Hard-boiled eggs (page 69–70)
B Opposite: Smoked trout (page 71)

manner, the floret is very small, and in proportion to the base upon which it rests. The next illustration, Fig. 67, shows how broccoli may be used as a component in a border design, with strips of red pimento linking the 'trees'.

Fig. 66 : A small broccoli branch as garnish
Fig. 67 : Broccoli as a border design

Cauliflower

This vegetable is not very popular for buffet work because of its neutral colour. However, tiny florets are effective against a dark background. They should first be blanched, then cut to the required size. To provide a somewhat brighter effect, dust the florets with a little paprika before arranging them. They may be used in a border pattern, as in Fig. 68, or as part of a 'bush' motif, with the florets as the blossom and shaped cucumber skin as the bush. In this case, use tiny cauliflower florets for the bush and insert tiny red dots cut from radish skin. Shape the trunk from cucumber skin.

Fig. 68 : Cauliflower border
Fig. 69 : Cauliflower 'bush'

Caviar

Genuine sturgeons' roe is seldom used these days for buffet work or for decoration because of its prohibitive cost. An alternative in terms of a decorative medium is either Danish or Swedish lumpfish roe. Both products are fish eggs and both are black, resembling genuine caviar in this respect at least. Try using this material to make a bunch of grapes (Fig. 70) to garnish any small piece of appropriate food – that is, any fish dish.

Fig. 70 : Lumpfish roe 'grapes'
Fig. 71 : Lumpfish roe representing earth

Fig. 72: A border for a whole salmon

Cut the vine stems from cucumber skin. Another way to use lumpfish roe is as an 'earth' base for a flower motif, Fig. 71. This type of background may be used in many other designs, and can be of particular interest when placed in the centre of a flower pattern, as it gives a particularly vivid contrast.

It is particularly useful when a border for a whole salmon is required, as shown in Fig. 72.

Capers

These grey-green pickled seeds are occasionally used in buffet decoration usually as part of a border pattern where the main motif requires a 'break' or a shape contrast. Capers are useful for this purpose, as are green peas and sweet corn.

Fig. 73: Capers alternating with main motif

Carrot

A colourful garnish, and one which may be used in a great many ways. Before being used as a decorative material, carrots should be three-quarters cooked in order to make them flexible, except when carrot 'curls' are to be made. Raw carrots are then used.

A carrot flower, is possibly one of the simplest decorations to make. Firstly, take a thin slice of carrot and cut it into eight equal segments

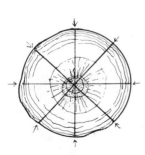

Fig. 74: Two stages towards a carrot flower

Fig. 75 : Carrot curls

(in half, in quarters, then cut again). These 'petals' are then opened up to produce the flower.

Carrot 'curls', often used as an appetiser, are made by slicing raw tender carrots very thinly with a vegetable peeler or a mandoline, curling the slices as if making a spring, and then securing them with a cocktail stick. They are then placed in iced water so they will hold their shape, and the cocktail sticks are removed before serving.

Celery

Celery stalks may be used to form many types of pattern and design, and a few ideas are shown below. To make celery curls (Fig. 76), the celery must not be too thick. Cut strips of tender celery to a length of about 4in (10cm), then make a number of slits at each end. Put in iced water for two hours to open cuts.

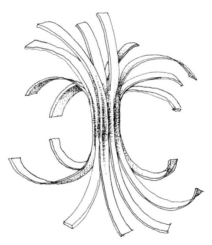

Fig. 76 : Celery curl

Two quite interesting ways to use celery as a component of a border pattern are illustrated below. In the first case, Fig. 77, the celery is cut to represent 'reeds'. Half-inch (1·5cm) pieces are cut very finely to within about $\frac{1}{8}$in (3mm) from the base and arranged at intervals along a 'bank' of chopped parsley. This makes an attractive border pattern against a dark background.

Cut celery may also be used as a raised petal motif. Cut the celery into thin strips and place in position (see Fig. 78) with curves of chive and a central spot of red pimento.

Fig. 77 : Celery reeds
Fig. 78 : Petal motif with celery, chive and red pimento

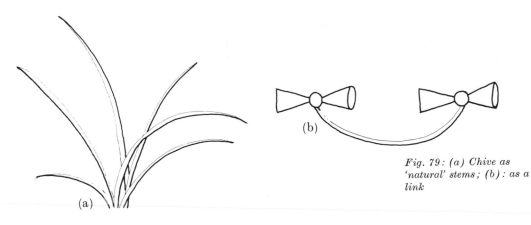

Fig. 79: (a) Chive as 'natural' stems; (b): as a link

Chive

Excellent for use as thin 'natural' stems for flowers, Fig. 79(a), or as a 'link' in a border pattern, (b). Blanch the stems for 2 minutes, then cool immediately in iced water before using.

Corn

A small can of sweet corn is useful to create decorative effects such as lemons on a branch, Fig. 80(a), fruit showing against a green leaf background (b), or as 'mimosa' on a large decorated piece. The kernels can also provide shape contrast in a border pattern, (c).

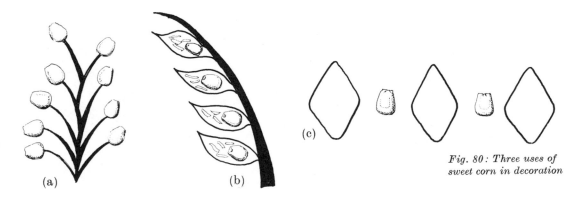

Fig. 80: Three uses of sweet corn in decoration

Cucumber

Should be firm and with symmetrical sides so that any slices used will be regular in diameter. Peeled and unpeeled cucumber is often grooved with the appropriate tool, or the same effect may be obtained by drawing the tines of a fork along the side. Then, when the cucumber is grooved, it may be sliced very thinly and the slices used either flat or as 'twists'.

Fig. 81: Grooves along the length of a cucumber

Fig. 82: Cucumber and carrot 'lily'

A cucumber lily is produced by folding a thin slice of cucumber around the base of a matchstick-shaped piece of carrot split into even thinner strips at the top, to form the stamen. A second slice of cucumber is placed on the opposite side, and the whole is kept in place by pushing a cocktail stick through the complete flower (Fig. 82).

Cucumber skin is most useful in many forms of decoration, as it can represent thick stems or firm and solid leaves in a most realistic way. For large platters of fish or meat, the skin can be cut to represent fern and used to decorate the edges of the platter.

Fig. 83: Cucumber skin 'fern'

Cucumber may also be used in a number of ways as a boat- or basket-shaped container for small savouries such as radishes or spring onions. To make a boat shape, take a small cucumber and slice a piece along the length so that it will set firmly on the table or platter. On the opposite side, cut off another piece lengthwise about one-third of the way down. Hollow out the cucumber and fill the cavity with small, colourful savouries, Fig. 84(a). Smaller baskets can be cut to carry items like asparagus tips, tiny carrots and so on, as illustration (b) shows.

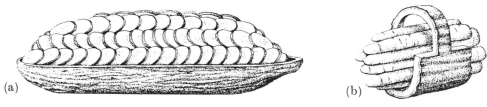

(a)

(b)

*Fig. 84: Cucumber containers.
(a): boat shape; (b): basket*

Cucumber 'flower cups' (see Fig. 85(a)) are made as follows: For each cup cut a 2in (5cm) length of cucumber and carefully hollow the seeds from one end to form a cup. Using a small, sharp knife cut the rind away in rounded petals (similar to those of a radish rose – see Fig. 100(a), page 54), starting about one-quarter of the way down from the top of the cup and cutting petals about 1in (2·5cm) long, without detaching them. Cut the top edge of the cucumber cup in scallops approximately the same size as the petals below, and set the cup in iced water to let the petals curl back. Fill the cups with any desired savoury mixture.

A cucumber 'chain' (see illustration (b)) is made as follows: Score the surface of an unpeeled cucumber with a vegetable decorating knife or by drawing the tines of a fork along its length. Cut the cucumber into slices about ⅛in (3mm) thick and remove the centre seeds without cutting the

(a) (b)

rind. If the cucumber is straight, this may be done with an apple corer
before slicing. Make one cut through the rind in all the slices except the
first ring. To form the chain, fit one ring into the other, opening and closing
each ring.

Decorative skewers

Decorative skewers add a distinctive touch to any large item on the buffet,
such as turkey, baked ham or ox tongue. They are inserted in the meat at
an angle for the best effect. Many colourful combinations can be worked
out and those shown below are very easy to prepare. The first, Fig. 86(a),
shows a glacé cherry, an artichoke heart, a stuffed olive and a tomato cup.
In (b) we have a cucumber coronet, a black olive, and a lemon cup. Notice
how well the dark and light colours are contrasted.

*Fig. 86: Simple decorative
skewers*

(a)   (b)

Eggs

Hard-boiled eggs are a valuable source of decoration. Chopped, sliced,
mashed or creamed, they can be used in many ways to provide accents of
white or deep yellow.

The white of hard-boiled egg is particularly useful if one wishes to produce a fast decoration on a large pâté or any flat surface. It takes the form
of a flower pot, and is done like this. Chop the egg whites finely and, with
a toothpick or the back of a small spoon, arrange them into a flower-pot
shape. Now take a strip of red pimento $\frac{1}{4}$in (6mm) wide and lay it flat
about one-third way down from the top of the flower pot, to form a band.

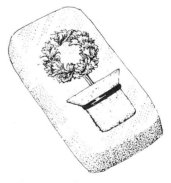

*Fig. 87: Hard-boiled egg
'flower pot'*

Take sprigs of parsley and arrange them in a circle above the flower pot, using the parsley stalk as the flower stem.

Gherkins

The most usual manner in which gherkins are shown is the simple 'fan'. Slice lengthwise, very thinly, to within ½in (1 cm) of the end and flatten with a knife-blade to make the fan.

Fig. 88: Gherkin 'fan'

Green beans

Fresh green beans, blanched and then cut into diamond shapes, can be used to represent leaves, or combined with other items to form part of a border pattern.

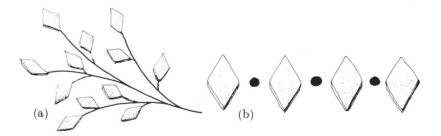

Fig. 89: Green beans as
(a): leaves;
(b): part of a border

(a)   (b)

Leek

The many different coloured leaves obtainable from one stem make this vegetable invaluable in providing many types of floral garnish. The illustrations (Fig. 90) show a few ways in which these leaves may be used, from a representation of a cedar tree to a simple curve.

Lemons

Very little need be said of the importance of lemons in decoration; there are so many ways they may be used. Some of the simpler ways to cut slices of lemon are shown in Fig. 91. In (a) a curl is made of the lemon rind attached to a half-slice. In (b), a butterfly shape is cut. A wedge with a pimento band is shown in (c), and (d) a Maltese cross.

In addition, lemon baskets make most attractive decorations. They are produced in the following manner: Mark out a 'handle' to run from one side

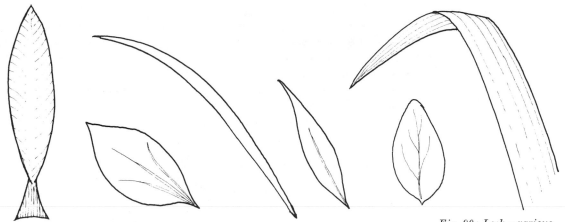

Fig. 90: Leek – various types of leaf motif

of the lemon to the opposite side, commencing half-way up the lemon, Fig. 92(a). Make another line to run around the lemon, commencing at the same point as the handle. Cut the two 'handle lines' first, then take the knife and cut from the sides of the lemon towards the handle lines (on both sides). *Be sure not to cut into the handle.* If desired, cut a serrated edge all round the rim. Take a thin slice from the base of the basket so that it will stand upright. Fill the basket with sprigs of parsley.

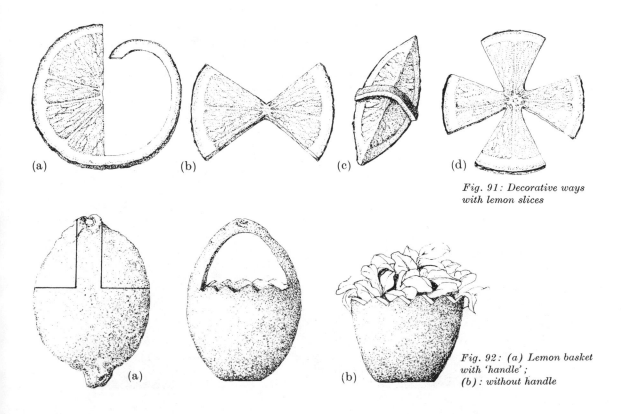

(a)   (b)   (c)   (d)

Fig. 91: Decorative ways with lemon slices

(a)   (b)

Fig. 92: (a) Lemon basket with 'handle'; (b): without handle

The other illustration, (b), shows a lemon basket without a handle. Make a serrated edge by cutting diagonal lines around the lemon, keeping the cuts even and making them deep, so that the knife reaches almost to the centre of the lemon. Twist the two halves to separate, and dress the exposed centres with parsley or watercress.

Slices of lemon may be made more attractive by garnishing them with radish 'spokes'. Cut four lines from the centre of the lemon slice and place thin slices of radish in the cuts (Fig. 93).

Fig. 93: Radish slices embellish a lemon base

Melon

The use of melon as a decorative aid is usually confined to its shell, which makes an ideal container for fruit salad, ice-cream or sorbet. When used in this manner it is a most attractive asset to the buffet table.

To make a basket with a handle, cut the melon in the same way as explained for Lemon Basket (Fig. 92(a)). In this case, the melon is cut into a boat shape. Another type of container may be made by standing the melon on end and propping up the top as a lid. To do this, cut the top off the melon, empty the seeds from the inside and scoop out the flesh with with a 'parisienne cutter'. Mix the melon balls with other ingredients for a fruit salad and pile it into the melon shell. Fix the lid as shown in Fig. 94(b) with a cocktail stick, so that the contents are clearly visible.

Fig. 94: (a) Melon basket with handle; (b): with lid

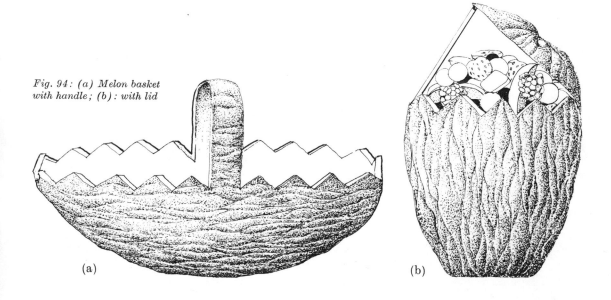

(a)

(b)

Mushroom

These are often used as a garnish, and usually the tiny button mushrooms are preferred. They are blanched prior to use and the curling underskin is pared. To prepare larger mushroom caps as a party food, blanch them for 1 minute, then chill. Pipe in the centre a 'star' of savoury cream and garnish with a small decoration in a contrasting colour.

Olives

All three types of olives are used in decoration: the green, the black and the stuffed olives. Black olives are very useful when a dark colour is needed as a contrast and, as with green olives, they may be sliced to form flower petals, stems and many other shapes. It is a good idea and a time saver, to buy de-stoned olives, but if they are not available the stones (pits) may be removed by cutting the olive length-ways and the two halves twisted gently to divide them. The stone may then be removed with the aid of a sharp knife. Below are a few decorative ideas using sliced olives. Illustration (a) shows slices of olive representing flower petals, with a piece of red pimento for the centre. In (b) half a black olive makes a flower pot, and overlapping slices the flower. For (c) slices of olive are paired on each side of a chive stem.

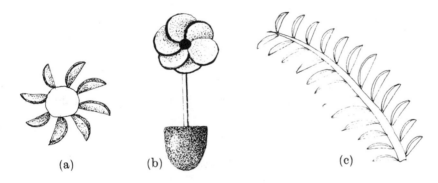

(a)　　　(b)　　　(c)

Fig. 95: Decorative designs using sliced olives

Stuffed olives, which have had the stone removed and the cavity filled with red pimento, are also very useful for decoration, and a few ideas are shown below. In design (a), pieces of red pimento top chive stems; in (b), strips of black olive form the petals, and in (c), a border design, chive forms the link.

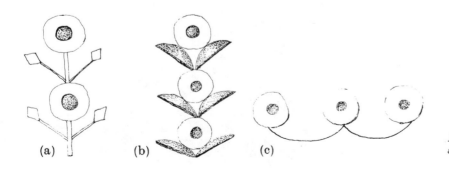

(a)　　　(b)　　　(c)

Fig. 96: Designs using stuffed olives

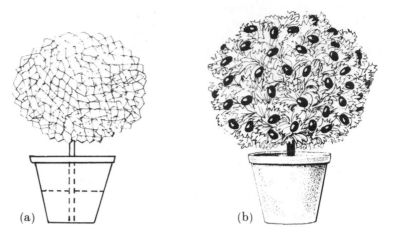

Fig. 97: Olive tree, materials assembled, and completed

(a)   (b)

Quite impressive table decorations may be made in the form of an 'olive tree'. You will require – a small plastic flower pot, a piece of polystyrene, some fine-gauge galvanised chicken wire and a stout wooden skewer, painted green. Put the polystyrene in the bottom of the flower pot, and stick the skewer firmly into it. Form the chicken wire into a rough spherical shape to represent the outline of a tree, and push it on to the other end of the skewer, as in Fig. 97(a). (You will have to put a 'pad' of some sort over the end of the skewer so it will not come through the chicken wire.) Now, with either green or black olives on cocktail sticks and sprigs of fresh parsley, construct your tree, as shown in illustration (b).

A very exotic presentation may be made on a similar principle, using shrimps and stuffed olives.

Fig. 98: Shrimp tree

To make a shrimp tree, fine-gauge chicken wire is shaped into a cone with the base splayed to make a firm foundation. Stuffed olives on cocktail sticks are placed in straight lines in the holes and each olive is encircled with a shrimp. Sprigs of parsley are inserted between each line of olives/shrimps to fill in any spaces, see Fig. 98.

Parsley

This is one of the most useful items in culinary decoration and may be used in many ways – chopped, sprigs, or in bunches as garnish for large pieces.

Peppers

Red, green and yellow peppers are used in decoration. The green pepper is most often used on the buffet table and, like the yellow pepper is bought fresh whereas most often the red variety is bought in tins. To use either green or yellow peppers, slice off the top and remove the internal membrane and seeds. Blanch for 5 minutes, then cool and use as required. The green pepper is ideal to represent thick, sturdy leaves or branches, and may also be cut and used as shaped decoration. Green and yellow pimentos are useful, too, as containers for cold sauces – mayonnaise, tartare, etc. – or virtually any other cold filling. There is no need to blanch the peppers when using them in this way. Slice off the top, remove the insides, then fill them with the sauce.

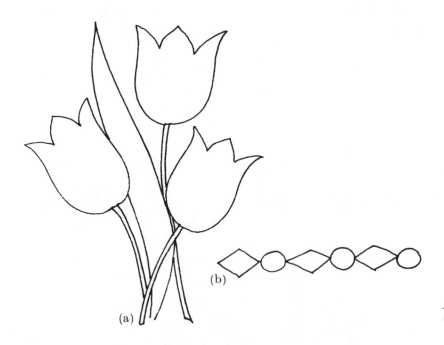

Fig. 99: (a) Tulip pattern;
(b): simple border pattern

Pimento

An excellent bright red decoration bought in cans. Strain off the packing liquor and open the pimentos so that they are flat. Cut into desired shapes. Because canned pimentos are quite large, they may be formed into substantial flower shapes, such as tulips (see Fig. 99) or poppies. Alternatively, small aspic cutters will help to give a positive design shape as part of a combined decoration. In Fig. 99 we see a simple border pattern with diamonds of red pimento alternating with green peas.

Radish

Radishes have a wide range of decorative uses. They may be cut into roses, polka-dots and fans, sliced thinly to form various shaped petals, flowers and other constituents of a design – in fact there are dozens of ways radish may be used.

Possibly the most important decoration is the *radish rose*, (Fig. 100(a)), produced in the following way. Cut off the roots of small red radishes and trim the stems, leaving a few of the inner leaves. With a thin, sharp knife peel the red skin away from the radish in 5 or 6 thin petals, starting from the root end and cutting $\frac{1}{4}$in (6mm) from the base, without detatching the skin. A second layer of petals may be cut under the first, if desired. Chill the roses in iced water for a few hours to open and curl the petals.

To make a *polka-dot*, illustration (b), trim small sections of the skin around the radish to obtain this effect.

For a *profile rose* design – (c) – a rose with 3 or 4 petals may be made. Cutting the radish in half, then lay the halves flat and cut out wedges as shown. A small piece of black is set at the base of each rose to represent the calyx.

For a *fan* – (d) – with a sharp knife cut oval radishes crossways 5 or 6 times without slicing all the way through. Chill the radishes in iced water for several hours so they will fan out. The cuts may be filled as desired with vegetable strips of a contrasting colour.

Radish 'profile' roses make most effective composite decorations, as Fig. 101 shows. Leek leaves are cut to shape and chive used for the stems.

Fig. 100(a): Radish rose; (b): polka-dot; (c): profile, (d): fan
Fig. 101: Radish 'profiles'

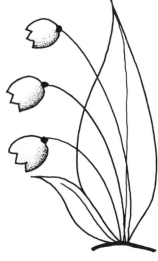

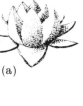
(a)

(b)

(c)

(d)

Tomatoes

Tomatoes are one of the favourite items used for decoration and garnish. Besides the simple floral pattern made with the outside trimmings (see Fig. 102(a)), tomatoes are very effective when cut into the shape of a water-lily, tomato baskets and tomato roses.

The *water-lily* is produced by making diagonal cuts from outside to centre. Twist to separate the two halves, then remove seeds and some of the flesh and fill as desired. The *basket* is made in a similar manner to the 'lemon basket' described on page 49.

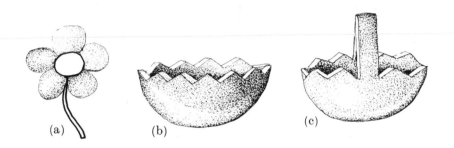

Fig. 102: Tomatoes in (a): Floral pattern; (b): water-lily; (c): basket

To make a *tomato rose* (a) take a sharp knife and, starting at the blossom end of a firm tomato, remove a 1in (2·5cm) strip of skin together with a thin layer of flesh, cutting around the fruit in a continuous spiral to the stem. Use a sawing motion, which will make the strip wavy, and be careful not to tear the skin. Holding the stem end of the strip in one hand, wind the strip around and around in a fairly tight ring until a rose shape is formed, keeping the bottom part of the flower a little tighter than the upper part. The petals should lean out, forming a wavy rose. Place the blossom on the platter and tuck a few leaves of watercress under it.

To make a *tomato rose* (b) – with the blossom end up, cut a small whole tomato into eight wedge-shaped sections, leaving the bottom quarter uncut. Spread the sections open. Run a knife behind each section to loosen the skin and a thin layer of flesh from the centre pulp. Re-shape the centre into its original round and sprinkle with a little sieved hard-boiled egg yolk.

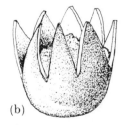

Fig. 103: Tomato roses

Turnips

A vegetable that is very often overlooked for use as decoration, turnip can be made into several flower shapes. For example, to make a *Calla lily*, cut very thin slices from the centre of a large white turnip. Make a cardboard pattern of the shape shown in Fig. 104(a) and trace it on to the slice of turnip. Cut out with a sharp knife. Roll the slice to the correct shape, insert a stamen made from a small trimmed carrot into the centre, and secure with a toothpick or thread. Chill in iced water. Leaves cut from the rind of a large cucumber will enhance the effect.

To make *jonquils*, draw a 6 petal pattern on cardboard as shown in (b). Lay the pattern on slices of white turnip. Trace and cut out with a sharp knife. Cut a small hole in the centre. From another thin slice, cut a strip about 2in (5cm) wide and make some fine slashes along one edge. Roll up and fasten at the back with a toothpick. Chill in iced water that has been coloured a deep yellow.

For a *dog-rose*, slice peeled white turnip about ⅛in (3mm) thick. Place cardboard tracing on the slice and cut out. Crisp the flowers in iced water. Some may be tinted red by colouring the water with carmine. Fasten a small sprig of parsley in the hole in the centre of the flowers.

For a *tulip*, smoothly peel medium-sized white turnips. Cut into slices of the desired thickness. Cut a pattern from cardboard, lay it on the slice, trace and cut out. (The stem and leaves may be cut from a cucumber rind – leek tops are good too.) To make a red tulip, soak the flower in water coloured with red vegetable dye. To prevent 'white flowers' made with turnip from discolouring after they have been made, dip them in a clear, warm (not hot) gelatine solution, then keep them in the refrigerator until required.

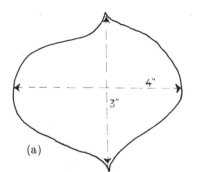

Fig. 104: Turnip designs. (a): Calla lily; (b): jonquil; (c): dogrose; (d): tulip

Tongue

The trimmings from salt tongue may often be usefully incorporated in a pattern when, for example, a little soft red colour is required. If their are large slices available, shapes may be cut out with aspic cutters.

Truffles

This item is not used to such a great extent today owing to its prohibitive cost. Needless to say, truffles give a beautiful black colour to any design. However, it is possible to make a fair facsimile by producing a gelatine sheet with a very black colour, as follows:

4 tablespoons truffle peelings
2 tablespoons unflavoured gelatine
6oz (150g) flavoured aspic jelly
1½ tablespoons dry sherry
a pinch of charcoal powder

Dissolve gelatine in aspic and combine with other ingredients in a blender
for 2 or 3 minutes. Heat the mixture for about 10 minutes in a *bain marie*
to emphasise the colour. Pour the liquid on to a slightly greased dish to
spread it in a very thin layer. Refrigerate until set.

Watercress
One of the most useful decorative aids, not only when used in small
bunches but also as single leaf or tiny sprig decorations on small items.

FREEHAND DESIGN

We have shown in the previous pages how simple yet attractive designs
may be made from various raw materials. Now let us discuss a more
difficult but interesting art – freehand designing.

Freehand designs are most often used on large, decorative pieces such
as hams, turkey, salmon, galantine and are most useful if one wishes to
carry a 'party theme' through to the main item of food on the buffet.
Designs of yachts for sailing club functions, rabbits and chicks for Easter
parties, and so on are not too difficult to produce.

There are two methods of producing this type of design:

1 by outlining the motif, then adding the internal detail;
2 by 'blocking' the motif, that is using a pattern or a cut-out, cutting
the material to shape, then adding the internal detail.

The optical result of both methods is shown below in Fig. 105.

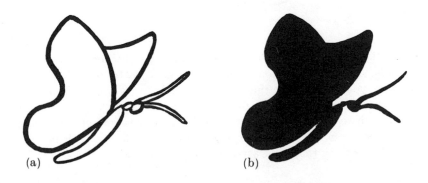

(a)   (b)

Fig. 105: Freehand designs.
(a): Outlined;
(b): blocked

As you will see, (a) shows an outline, and when placed upon any background (such as a *chaudfroid*) the body will show the colour of the back-

ground. In example (b), the butterfly will have the colour of the material from which it is cut. Example (a) gives a more delicate effect, while example (b) is very much easier to achieve.

Design by Outline

In some kitchens this type of design is still made with thinly-sliced truffle, cut to resemble string and providing an excellent contrast when placed against a *chaudfroid* background. However, an alternative may be used, such as the 'truffle sheet' made with gelatine, or, for that matter, the blanched skin of *aubergine*. To obtain your motif, trace the chosen design on to a piece of greaseproof paper and put it on the work table. Now, over this drawing place a piece of clear, thin glass. Make sure that the glass is *larger* that the design and gives a good overlap. Pour a little *clear* aspic over the glass to cover the whole design. Allow this to set. When ready, cut the truffle sheet into very thin strips, like string, using a very sharp knife or a single-sided razor blade, and with a pair of tweezers pick up the strings and place them over the outline of the design. When you are cutting the 'strings', remember to try to follow the contour of the design: for example, if you are following the curve of a butterfly wing, cut sufficient of the black aspic to a similar curve. This will help the outline fall neatly and without too many rough corners. When the outline has been completed, apply another coat of *clear* aspic (this time with a small, very soft brush) over the outline to hold the black strings in place. Allow to set.

Fig. 106: Finished 'outline' butterfly

When the aspic is firm, take a spatula and, gently lifting the whole 'sandwich', slide it into position on the food item or platter to be decorated. Just before you do this, give the background a light coating of clear aspic so that the design will stay in place. The outline design may then be finished off in an appropriate manner. One simple idea is to cut tiny 'new moon' shapes from red pimento or, continuing with the black theme, cut similar shapes from the black aspic and put in position.

The Cut-out Method

A pattern is made from cardboard and placed over the material to be used

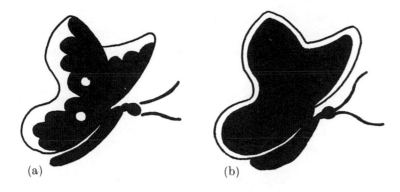

(a)   (b)

Fig. 107: Cut-out method with
(a): Internal contrast;
(b): outline contrast

– 'truffle aspic' or red pimento, for example. The pattern is then cut and lifted with a pair of tweezers, dipped in clear aspic and placed on the background. Internal details are then added. With a pimento butterfly, a good contrast would be 'new moon' shapes cut from the white of a hard-boiled egg. For even greater contrast one may combine both methods in this manner. The cut-out design is placed in position on the background. Then the outline of the cut-out is followed and 'strings' of a contrasting colour are added. For example, should the butterfly be blocked out with red pimento, you may decide that a good contrast would be to outline the cut-out design with strings of black aspic.

Aspic Painting

Perhaps the most difficult method of decorating with aspic is freehand painting, but of course this skill allows much more freedom of expression. It is in effect a combination of the outline work explained previously, and finishing off by freehand painting. The Chinese trees illustrated here are produced in this manner.

An 'outline design' is produced and placed on the background. Clear aspic is prepared and coloured as required. The clear aspic is put into egg-cups and appropriate colours are added, in the form of various vegetable dyes. This is the 'aspic paint'. It must be kept in a sticky but fluid state, and it is a good idea to place the egg-cups in a *bain-marie* to keep the

Fig. 108: Painting in aspic – Chinese tree

coloured aspic sufficiently free-running.

The aspic is applied with a paint brush and the attraction of this type of work is that the most beautiful 'shadings' may be produced, particularly with flower painting, and in this manner a much more subtle effect is obtained.

With the Chinese trees (Fig. 108), the outline was in black aspic strings, and the blossom was painted in two shades of pink. The leaves were in two shades of green – light and dark – on the other. You can imagine just what a beautiful picture it made.

4

Appetisers,
Hors-d'œuvre, Salads and Soups

Appetisers

On any buffet there are always a number of items which can be termed 'tantalising titbits'. Appetisers and other items for 'nibbling' can be either extremely simple or as elaborate as you choose. In most cases it is better to err on the side of simplicity, and concentrate on obtaining a good finish of the product.

Appetisers that are to be served as cocktail or pre-buffet accompaniments should be small, tasty and easy to eat. They should be attractive to the eye and the palate and yet not hearty and filling. Food of this type is meant to coax the appetite, not to appease it. Foods that are designed to be eaten in one or two bites should be manageable, hold together well when picked up and should not drip. Foods prepared to be served on a cocktail stick should be firm enough to hold on the pick.

In planning an assortment, avoid too many similar types. Include at least one unusual, impressive offering that will become the talking point of the occasion. Aim to have everything you serve distinctive in its own right. Even the most familiar items can be very successful if you present them just a little differently.

Appetisers need to be piquant, otherwise they lose much of their point. But colour and texture are issues that deserve careful thought: garnishes and arrangement are as important as any other consideration.

Many simple cocktail items, including salted nuts, potato crisps and salted crackers, are bought in packets and are very useful as fillers for the buffet table and bar. In addition, of course, it is often necessary to produce other items from your own kitchen.

Dips

Dips are very easy to make, and have the advantage that they can be mixed in advance; in fact, the bulk of the work falls upon the guests. Bowls of these soft, well-seasoned mixtures attractively arranged and displayed in interesting containers, with assorted biscuits and crisps to allow the guests to help themselves are always popular.

By far the most popular dips are those made from cream cheese. There is a basic recipe for this type of dip, and by adding a variety of different flavourings, many excellent bowls can be produced. *Basic recipe:* To every 1lb (450g) of cream cheese add 4 tablespoons of double cream. Beat well and add any of the following:

2 tablespoons chopped chive and 1 tablespoon Danish Blue cheese.
2 tablespoons chopped dates and 2 teaspoons grated orange peel.
2 tablespoons crisped, crumbled bacon, a little minced onion and the mashed yolk of one hard-boiled egg.
2 dessertspoons anchovy paste and 2 teaspoons chopped parsley.
2 dessertspoons bloater paste plus the rind and juice of lemon.

Of course, to make the table attractive, your appetisers, 'nibbles', sauces and dips must be shown off in interesting containers. Try some of these.

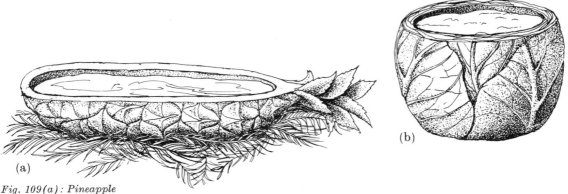

(a)

(b)

Fig. 109(a): Pineapple shell container;
(b): hollowed cabbage

Half a scooped pineapple set upon natural fern is ideal for a savoury dip or a sauce, or hollow out the centre of a round cabbage, preferably one with curly leaves, or a red cabbage. Stand a container of sauce or a savoury dip in the centre.

To make a 'pin cushion' from a globe artichoke, cut across the top. Stick assorted appetisers in the centre. Keep the colours different.

Appetisers on Sticks

Of all types of appetiser, probably none offers more scope than the modern variety presented on cocktail sticks. Try some of these combinations:

Melon balls wrapped in ham
A cube of cheese with a fresh green or black grape
Cube of hard cheese with a glacé cherry
Cheese with a stuffed olive
Cheese and a mandarin or orange segment

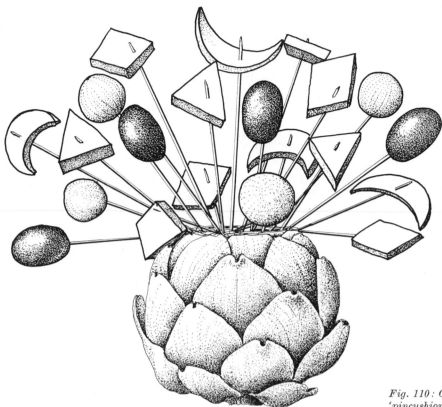

Fig. 110 : Globe artichoke 'pincushion'

Cheese and a small pineapple wedge
White cocktail onion and a slice of frankfurter
Melon ball between two thin squares of ham
Cubes of lamb tongue and wafer-thin slice of carrot
Slices of ham, rolled and cut into 1in (2·5cm) lengths
Raw mushroom caps filled with sardine spread
Artichoke hearts cut in half on a cube of cheese
Stoned dates wrapped in ham or salami
Blanched cauliflower florettes on a cube of corned beef
Stoned dates stuffed with cream cheese and pineapple mixture
Assorted canapés (see appropriate section) cut into 1in (2·5cm) pieces

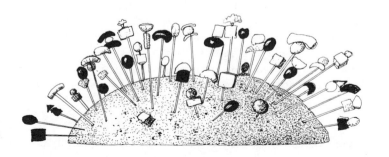

Fig. 111: A cocktail 'hedge-hog' – half an aubergine

Fig. 112: Cocktail appe-
tisers

These and other varieties of appetisers may be presented on a grape-fruit 'hedgehog' or, to obtain a different effect, you could use half an aubergine or a very large potato as a base.

Raw vegetables, cut in sticks or in florets are low in calories and high in appeal. They add a handsome splash of colour as well as a refreshing crunch.

Small pastry turnovers, about 1in (2·5cm) across, are a welcome addition to any party when they are served piping hot. Fill them with creamed chicken, fish, ham, cheese or chicken livers. Try serving very small wedges of pizza or quiche lorraine.

Bacon-wrapped savouries are great favourites. Here again the possibilities for variety of filling are considerable. Thin slices of streaky bacon are 'stretched' with the back of a knife, cut into 1in (2·5cm) slices and may be wrapped around such items as chicken livers; tiny tinned oysters; shrimps; cocktail sausage; pineapple chunks or button mushrooms. They are grilled or pan-fried just before serving, put on cocktail sticks and brought to the table.

It is advisable to have the service staff circulate among the guests with the trays of hot savouries. This will ensure that the guests will eat them while they are still at least warm and palatable. Heated savouries served cold lose all their appeal.

An interesting method of presenting cold bites served on cocktail sticks is to make a 'parsley tree' like the one shown in Fig. 97, on page 52; instead of putting stuffed olives in the chicken wire, you can insert the spiked cocktail savouries. Allow the stick to come right through the food items so that the guests can easily remove them from the tree – the sticks should protrude about $\frac{1}{2}$in (1cm). Be sure to cover the wire with plenty of parsley so that the tree does not look too bare once guests start eating.

Potato Baskets
Another pleasing food container may be produced from very thinly sliced

Opposite: Combination individual and platter salads (page 72–6)

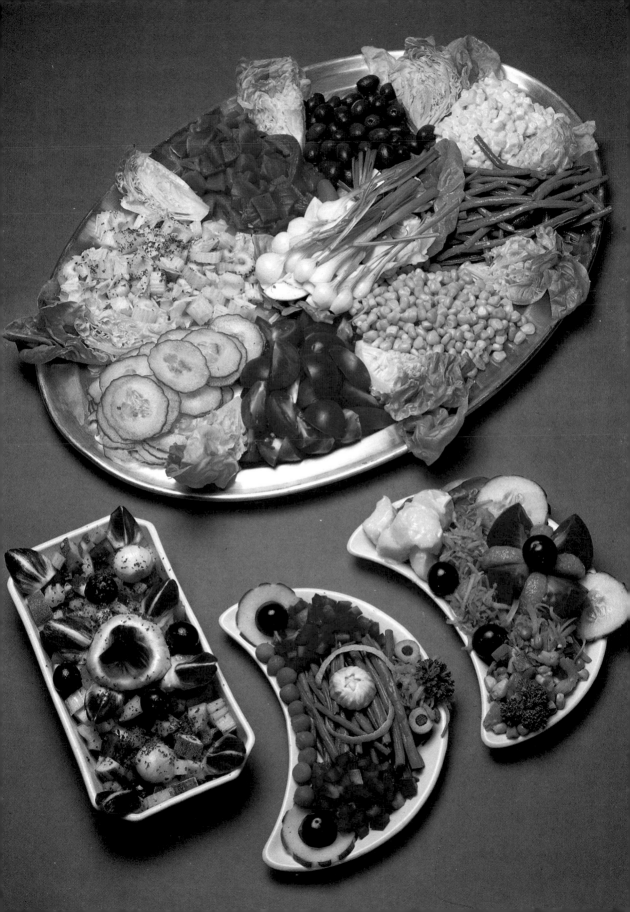

potato fashioned to form a nest. To make these nests you will need two round wire sieves with fairly coarse mesh. If possible, one should be about $\frac{3}{4}$in (2cm) larger in diameter than the other. Peel some large potatoes, then slice them very thinly, either by hand or on the 'mandoline'. Soak the slices in cold water for 1 hour. It is most important that the slices are as thin as possible so they will take the shape of the strainer without breaking. Place the large strainer (sieve) in very hot deep-fat to become well heated and greased. Arrange the slices of potato in the bowl of the strainer, overlapping them to make an attractive pattern. Then place the smaller strainer in the hot fat and push it firmly on top of the potato slices in the larger strainer. The slices are thus clamped between the two bowls, as in Fig. 113(a). The nest is kept in position by holding the two wire handles during the cooking in the hot fat. When the potatoes are golden brown, carefully remove the top strainer and gently ease the potato nest out of the larger strainer.

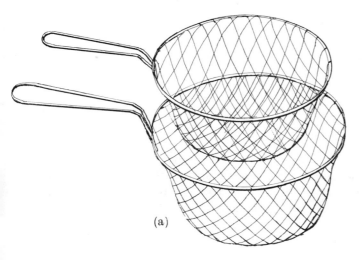

(a)

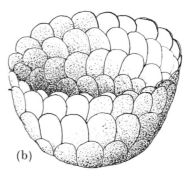

(b)

Fig. 113(a): The two strainers used to make (b): a potato basket

Pastry Containers
To add interest to the buffet table, various types of pastry container may be used with effect.

Barquettes
These are simply pastry boats made by lining the appropriate shaped tins with savoury short-crust and baking them 'blind'. Allow to cool and then fill with your own choices of savoury filling. Decorate as required. If you decide to use a strip decoration, have the filling raised above the edge of the case. If you will use a tiny floral decoration, spread the filling quite flat so that there is an even surface to work on.

Suggested Fillings
Caviar boats Danish caviar (lumpfish roe) and finely chopped egg white

Opposite: Pâté with 'truffle' decorations (page 56–7)

mixed with a little mayonnaise, thick cream and lemon juice. Top with sieved yolk.

Sardine and cheese   Mashed sardines, lemon juice. Top with grated Parmesan or Gruyère cheese.

Tuna   Mix fish with chutney till smooth. Garnish with prawns and strips of red pepper.

Devilled ham   Minced ham with cream. Add a little chutney or curry powder.

Crab and tomato   Mix crab meat with cream and tomato purée (or tomato sauce). To make a more economical mixture use equal quantities of chopped hard-boiled egg.

Tartelettes   Similar to 'barquettes' except for the shape. When filled with an appropriate mixture they may be decorated in the same way.

Cornets   Most often made with short-crust when used on a buffet. Should not be more than 2in (5cm) long. Remember that cornets are displayed on their side and therefore any filling must be somewhat stiff to hold its shape. Decoration may be added in the mouth of the cornet if desired.

Bouchée   Made with puff-pastry and should be no longer than $\frac{3}{4}$in (7cm) in diameter. May also be made with choux paste. After baking the case may be cut in half across, the desired filling put on to the base and then covered with the top, or the filling may be piped into the bouchée through a small hole made in the side of the crust with the piping tube.

Carolines   Tiny éclair-shaped cases made with choux paste and piped out to a maximum length 1$\frac{1}{2}$in (3·5cm). They are often piped into the shape of a 'C', and sometimes in a circle. When cool, slice off the top, place the filling on the base and cover with the top.

Caisses   These rather elaborate 'food containers' are made from stale loaves. They can be made from almost any shape of loaf, but oblong (sandwich) loaves are easier to use.
  Cut the crusts from the loaf and make a *lid* by cutting *into* the loaf with a sharp knife about 1in (2·5cm) from the top. Drop the whole shape into

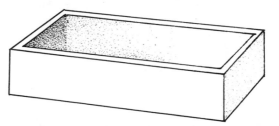

Fig. 114: 'Caisse' container

very hot deep-fat and cook until the sides are nicely brown. Remove and drain well. Gently lift the 'lid' (which will come away easily from the top). With the knife remove the centre of the loaf, leaving a wall about ½in (1cm) all round. If preferred, the *caisse* may be brushed with butter or some other fat all over and put into a very hot oven to brown. When cool, almost anything may be displayed in this bread container, providing of course it is fairly dry. It is most often used for small party sandwiches.

DECORATIVE HORS – D'ŒUVRE FOR BUFFETS

In this section we will show some interesting methods of presenting the more common type of *hors-d'œuvre*.

Avocado
The bland but delicate flesh from this fruit needs to be served with a sharp, somewhat acid contrast to bring out the true flavour and richness of the pulp. The avocado has a natural affinity with shellfish of any sort, and therefore the following fillings may be of interest.

Cubed avocado served in a glass with:
Diced cooked lobster, with mayonnaise and a little tomato sauce
Flaked crabmeat, French dressing and a dash of Worcestershire sauce
Shrimps with mayonnaise, tomato sauce and lemon juice

Avocado in the shell served with:
Shrimp and mayonnaise
Jellied consommé
Chicken julienne, mayonnaise, chopped celery and black olives
Fresh fruit: strawberry, black and green grapes and a dash of caster sugar

Avocado cream Split the avocado remove the stone and scoop out the pulp with a spoon, leaving sufficient flesh to keep the sides from falling. Finely mince the pulp, add a little single cream and tomato ketchup and mix until smooth. Replace mixture in shell and garnish with diced cucumber or diced melon. Serve very cold.

Avocado Waldorf Dice the avocado flesh and add equal parts of diced apple, diced cooked new potatoes and sliced celeriac. Mix with a little fresh lemon juice and a touch of sugar, a sprinkle of nutmeg and the smallest pinch of ground clove. Pile into the shell, pour a little fresh single cream over the whole and garnish with two peeled walnuts.

Avocado with smoked salmon Scoop the flesh with a parisienne cutter to make small balls. Take the required number of slices of salmon and place three avocado balls on each slice. Roll the smoked salmon around the balls and see that the 'join' of the fish rests underneath so the presentation keeps its shape. Serve on a lettuce leaf.

Grapefruit

Grapefruit are so good and so popular that they are served as an appetiser more often than any other fruit. Here are two simple and fast ideas. Cut the grapefruit to make a scalloped edge, then with a grapefruit knife separate the flesh from the skin. Sugar the flesh if necessary. Garnish with 4 sections of fresh orange and finish off with a cherry in the centre.

Fig. 115: Grapefruit with orange segments

For a Poinsettia effect, cut 12 thin, unpeeled slices of red apple. Press the slices between the cut grapefruit sections to resemble poinsettas. Grapefruit segments served with another fruit and presented in the form of a 'wheel' is a simple but effective idea. Here are some examples:

Alternate segments of grapefruit with similar segments of avocado pear. Put a little mayonnaise in the centre of the wheel and top with a small black olive

Grapefruit segments alternated with fresh apple segments, mayonnaise in centre, top with green olive

Grapefruit segments alone, mayonnaise in centre with 4 small shrimps in form of a cross

Grapefruit segments alternated with orange sections, mayonnaise in centre criss-crossed with strip of red pepper and green pepper.

These 'wheel' arrangements should be served on a bed of lettuce or watercress leaves.

Melon

The more usual way to serve this fruit is to cut it into sections, cut the flesh from the skin and slice the flesh into bite-sized pieces. The garnish is often a glacé cherry and a sprig of fresh mint, or perhaps a small bunch of frosted grapes. (To frost grapes first dip them in unbeaten egg white and shake to remove excess, then sprinkle with granulated sugar.) Two unusual ideas for service are:

Fig. 116: Melon ring filled with fruit

Melon with port Slice off the top of the melon and remove the seeds. Empty a glass of good port, Madeira or other fortified wine into the cavity. Replace the lid and keep chilled for an hour or so. Pour out the wine, then slice the melon into sections as usual.

Melon rings Cut the melon across into slices about 1in (2·5cm) thick. Remove the seeds from each slice, then fill the hole with fresh fruit piled high. Garnish with a sprig of leaves.

Hard-boiled Eggs

Decorated eggs can be easy to prepare and are certainly a food for a festive occasion. They may be served simply with a savoury filler, such as sardine or blue cheese combined with the mashed yolk and seasonings, or they may be made an important part of the buffet by the addition of decoration.

The most usual way to serve stuffed eggs is to cut them lengthways (after they have been shelled, of course). The yolks are removed and may be mixed with the following ingredients which should be piled high in the white cases, to give a lavish effect:

Mashed sardines, chopped chive, salt and pepper to taste, and a little mayonnaise. Mix well and pipe the mixture into the white shell. Sprinkle with paprika.

Canned salmon and a little prepared mustard and mayonnaise to bind. Pipe into shells and garnish with a sprig of parsley.

A little Danish caviar, or 'lumpfish' roe. Garnish with a sprinkling of finely chopped onion and grated rind of lemon.

A little crabmeat, mayonnaise and some minced onion.

Minced chicken in mayonnaise and minced black olive. Garnish with a small sprig of celery leaf.

For more important occasions, fill the shell in the normal manner, but keep the mixture level with the egg white shell. Then try some of these garnishes:

Fig. 117(a): Asparagus with band of red pimento; (b): 4 slices of radish embedded in the mixture; (c): Tiny tomato slice and stuffed olive; (d): Stuffed olive flower, chive stem; (e): Maltese cross from cucumber, radish dot centre; (f): Sprigs of watercress, black olive centre

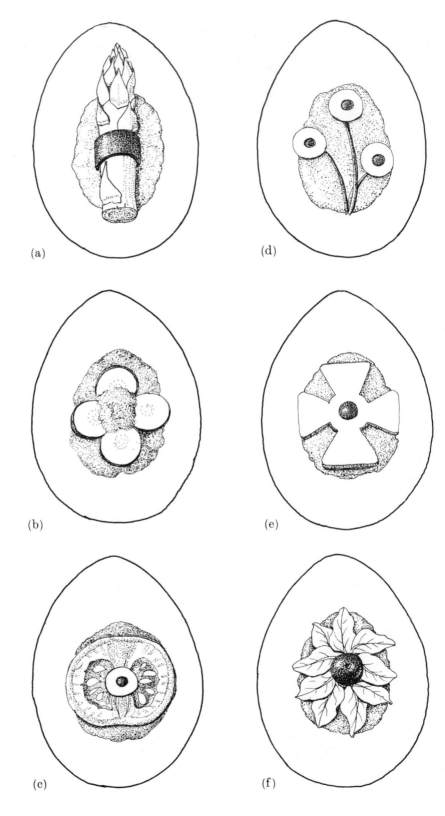

(a)

(d)

(b)

(e)

(c)

(f)

For very special presentations, you may care to decorate the side of a whole hard-boiled egg. To do this, brush the sides of the egg with aspic, have your decorations ready cut, then place them in position on the side of the egg. Set the egg in the refrigerator. Just prior to service lightly brush over the decoration with aspic to give a glossy finish. Chill for 15 minutes before bringing to the table. Use tiny pieces of radish, olive, diamonds of cucumber for the flowers and thin stalks of chive for the stems. Cut a slice from the base of the hard-boiled egg to allow it to stand upright on the service dish.

Smoked Trout

Most often served with horseradish cream. You may like to try simple presentation. Firstly remove the skin from the centre section of the fish, then decorate with a tiny floral design and brush with aspic.

Another attractive service method is to fillet the trout, decorate with a tiny floral design and lightly glaze with aspic. Prepare a tomato cup, fill it with horseradish cream and garnish with two small wedges of lemon – see Fig. 118(b).

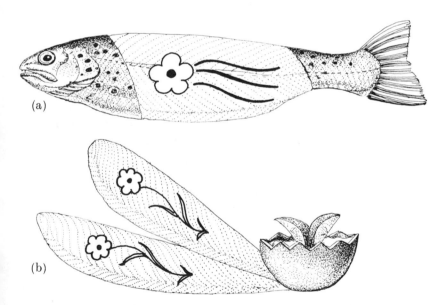

(a)

(b)

Fig. 118: Two ways to decorate trout: (a): Whole; (b): filleted

Smoked Salmon

This most popular *hors d'œuvre* is usually served in very thin slices and garnished with wedges of lemon. There are a few alternatives to this method of service. One is to roll two asparagus tips in each slice and decorate each roll with half black olive. Another is to form the slice into a cornucopia or horn of plenty and fill the cavity with potted shrimps. But a very unusual presentation is to form the smoked salmon slices into a rose. The method is as follows:

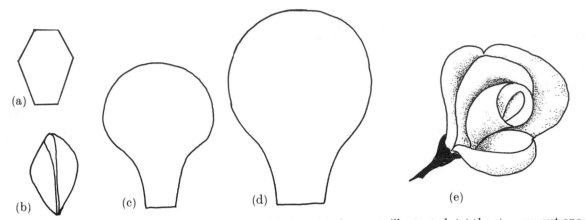

(a)

(b)

(c)

(d)

(e)

Fig. 119: Smoked salmon rose, the stages in making

Cut the slice of fish into the shapes as illustrated. (a) the stamen, cut one; (c) the smaller petals, cut three; (d) the large petal, cut one.

Roll the small piece of salmon (a) into a 'stamen' as shown (b) and then wrap the smaller petals around this centre. Finally, the single large petal is wrapped around the rest of the flower, and the petals are turned back slightly to give a realistic effect (e). The rose is garnished with leaves from cucumber skin or leek.

COMBINATION SALADS

An almost essential part of a buffet table is a colourful and attractive salad. There are two types commonly used – combination salads and salad platters. The former are presented in salad *bowls* and are composite salads, containing items other than vegetables, while the latter are shown on flat dishes or platters, and by the arrangement of vegetables of which they are exclusively composed, form a pattern or design. Here are a few ideas for attractive and inexpensive combination salads:

Alsace　Sliced potatoes and a few artichoke bottoms, seasoned with a little oil and tarragon vinegar and sprinkled with finely chopped chervil. Arrange in a dome in the bowl and decorate with a criss-cross of anchovy fillets. Arrange a border of tomato wedges and green olives.

Argenteuil　Heaped diced potato seasoned with mayonnaise and a little chopped chervil. Decorate the mound of potatoes with asparagus tips, and garnish the border with shredded lettuce and slices of hard-boiled egg.

Astoria　Dome of cooked rice seasoned with a little oil, paprika and chopped onion, then sprinkled with chopped parsley. Border of alternate quarters of tomato and pieces of green pepper.

Brilat　Equal quantities of diced potato and cooked green peas, moistened with mayonnaise seasoned with a little curry powder. Surround with prawns or shrimps and stuffed olives in small heaps, separated from each other by quarters of hard-boiled egg.

Creole   Prepare and cook green, red and yellow peppers, then chop them separately. Mix each colour with cooked, seasoned rice and arrange in separate mounds. Garnish each mound with a sprinkle of chopped chives and surround the bowl with alternate slices of tomato and cucumber.

Du Barry   Florets of cauliflower cooked *au point* and garnished with tiny radishes and sprigs of watercress.

Duchesse   Diced potato and julienne of celery mixed with chopped green peppers. Bind with mayonnaise and form into a mound. Decorate the border with triangles of ham, tongue or liver sausage. Decorate the top with a circle of sliced green pepper and place a radish rose inside the circle.

Flemish   Chicory and sliced potato moistened with a little vinaigrette dressing, in a dome, garnished with thin strips of rollmop herring. Sprinkle with chopped parsley.

Gala   A dome of cooked rice seasoned with a little French dressing and mixed with crabmeat. Surround with blanched diced celeriac and quartered tomatoes.

Italian   Mix equal quantities of potato, carrot, tomato and green beans, roughly chopped and bound with mayonnaise. Shape into a dome and garnish with anchovy fillets cut into small pieces. Surround with alternate slices of tomato and cucumber.

Palais Royal   Mix sliced potato, sliced eating apples and green beans with a little mayonnaise and arrange in a dome. Surround the dome with wedges of lettuce and quartered hard-boiled eggs.

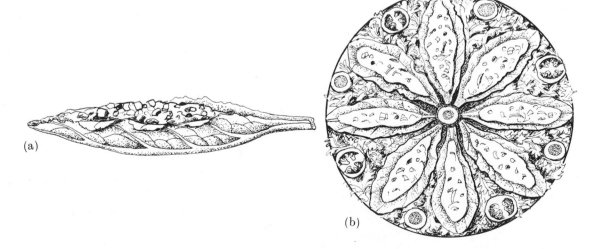

(a)

(b)

Fig. 120: Salad Patricia.
(a): Served on a lettuce leaf;
(b): arranged on a dish

Patricia   Use the leaves of a cos lettuce (romaine) as long, boat-shaped containers for each portion of salad. Mix equal parts of chopped green beans, green peas and potatoes with a little chopped red pepper. Bind with mayonnaise and place in the lettuce leaves. Arrange on a flat dish; the borders may be decorated with alternate quartered hard-boiled egg and sliced tomato. Parsley sprigs are positioned between the individual lettuce leaves.

Fig. 121: Oval platters

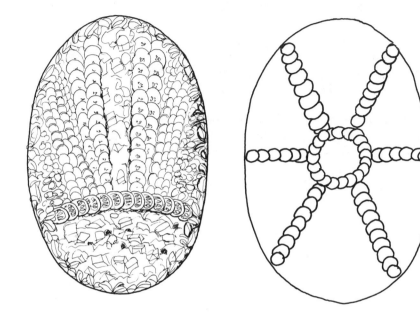

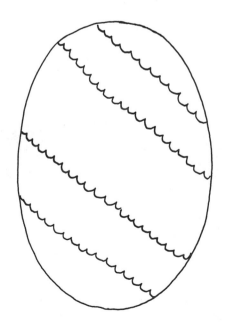

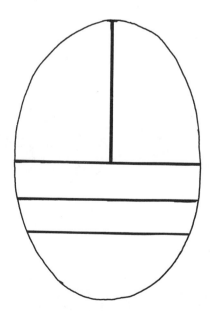

DECORATIVE PLATTERS

There are a number of occasions when salads need to be presented on platters or trays, rather than in the more conventional bowls. On these occasions it is always a good idea to arrange the vegetables in 'sections' so that at the outset, they may add to the colourful presentation of the buffet, and guests may help themselves to the different sections.

There is of course a variety of ways in which these platters may be decorated and an almost infinite number of designs that can be produced. In the following illustrations of decorative salad platters you will notice that the design of each platter emphasises the 'form' (or shape) of the dish itself. Also notice that the constituents of each platter contrast in colour, shape and texture.

Vegetable Permutations

The following is a list of the different types of vegetables that may be used in a decorative platter, and the various forms in which they may be cut. When this permutation is considered in relation to the patterns that can be made, it can be seen that producing these decorative platters is an exciting and interesting exercise.

RAW VEGETABLES	COLOUR	SHAPE			
		Circles	Dice	Strips	Bunch
Cabbage	Red			x	
Celeriac	White	x	x	x	
Celery	White			x	
Chicory	White			x	
Cress	Green				x
Cucumber	Green	x	x	x	
Curly endive	Green			x	x
Lettuce	Green			x	x
Olive	Black	x	x		
Olive	Green	x	x		
Onions, spring	Green	x	x	x	x
Parsley	Green			x	x
Peppers	Green	x	x	x	
Peppers	Red	x	x	x	
Peppers	Yellow	x	x	x	
Radish	Red	x	x		
Tomatoes	Red	x	x		
Watercress	Green			x	x

COOKED OR BLANCHED VEGETABLES	COLOUR	SHAPE			
		Circles	*Dice*	*Strips*	*Bunch*
Artichoke bottom	Green		x	x	
Asparagus	Green			x	x
Aubergine	Mauve	x	x	x	
Broccoli	Green			x	x
Carrots	Orange	x	x	x	
Cauliflower	White				x
Courgettes	Green	x	x	x	
French beans	Green		x	x	x
Leeks	White	x	x	x	
Mushrooms	Brown	x	x		
Parsnips	White	x	x	x	
Peas	Green	x			
Potatoes	White	x	x	x	
Sprouts	Green				x

MOULDED SALADS

Among the less common types of salad served on a buffet, but one which is tremendously popular in the United States and Canada, is the moulded salad, using gelatine as a binding agent.

An advantage of moulded salads is that they can be made from almost any pieces of food that have been left over, so they are economical to produce as well as lending themselves to very decorative treatment. In addition, of course, they may be made a day in advance of the function and kept in the refrigerator until needed.

Moulded salads are made from unflavoured gelatine dissolved in heated vegetable or fruit juices or in diluted cream soups of various kinds. When soup is used as the liquid agent, the moulded salad will of course not be clear. Before we discuss the methods of production – just a few words about gelatine.

There are a number of brands on the market and the strength varies from one to another. It is essential therefore to follow the manufacturer's instructions regarding the amount of liquid to use. Remembering this, there is just one more point – as you will be adding vegetables, fish, meat or fruit to the gelatine in considerable quantities (in relation to the amount of 'jelly') you should reduce the recommended amount of liquid by *one-tenth,* but no more. A reduction of too much liquid will make the gelatine tough. The gelatine should be fragile and tender. It will break easily if improperly handled. It should be tender enough to quiver and shake when transferred to a plate.

Use of Fruit or Syrup from Canned Fruits

Do not discard the syrup or juice from canned fruit. Save it to add to the

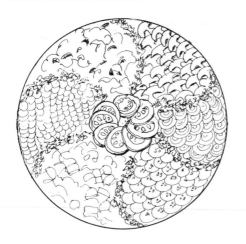

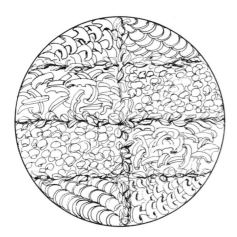
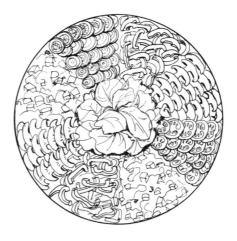

Fig. 122: Round platters

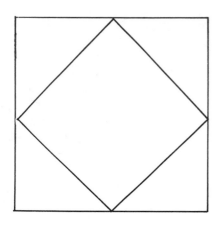

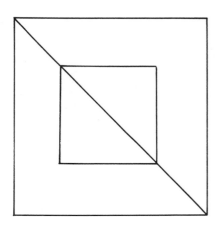

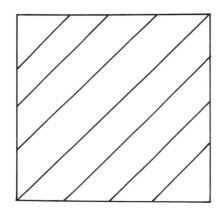

Fig. 123: Square platters

liquor you will use to make the gelatine mould. Take care that the syrup is not discoloured or that the colour will not detract from the desired effect of the moulded salad.

Most fruit juices may be used directly with gelatine. The exception is fresh or frozen pineapple juice which must be *boiled* (not just heated), then cooled slightly before mixing with the gelatine. Enzymes in the juice are thereby killed, and do not destroy the 'setting' quality of the gelatine.

To Make a Moulded Salad

Anodised ring moulds are the most convenient receptacle in which to make a moulded salad. Of course, any shaped mould may be used, providing that it is appropriate to the filling. Don't use a mould shaped like a fish and fill it with chicken! One important thing to remember when making any kind of moulded salad: dip the mould in cold water, drain but do not dry, before putting in the food or pouring the gelatine. This practice will make the jelly mixture easier to remove when set.

The simplest way to produce a salad very quickly is as follows: Allow about 12oz (325g) of solids to each ½ pint (300ml) of liquid gelatine. Drain and chill all foods, then pile *fairly loosely* into the mould. Just as the gelatine mixture thickens to about the consistency of unbeaten egg-white, whisk it while still in the pan to break up any large pieces, then pour it over the contents in the mould. The thickening gelatine will find its own way down to the bottom of the mould, if you give it a shake and a little physical help. Leave it to rest and get into the nooks and crannies of the food for about 10 minutes, then put in the refrigerator to set firm.

This is the method if you are making a moulded salad of, say, *macedoine* of vegetables, chopped chicken and peas, or in fact any salad that does not require an internal decoration. A great many of the moulded salads are of this type, firstly because they are quick and easy to produce, and secondly they are a most attractive yet extremely economical party piece.

Should you wish to provide a more elaborate salad, with a transparent, decorated top, then the procedure is slightly different. A small amount of liquid gelatine is poured into a well-chilled mould, and is rolled around the interior until the inside surface is coated with a thin layer. The mould is then put back into the refrigerator to allow the gelatine to set. To decorate the interior, pierce each piece of food you are intending to use as the top decoration with a cocktail stick, dip them one by one into the liquid gelatine in the saucepan, then place them in position in the mould. The cold gelatine on the bottom and sides will help the decorative items to set in place quickly. When the layer of decoration is in place, cover with more gelatine to hold them firmly in position and return the mould to the refrigerator to set firmly. After the designs have set, the centre of the mould may be filled with various types of meat, fish, poultry, diced cheese, etc, then topped up with gelatine to seal it and finish off the mould.

A popular way to present ring-moulded salads is to have them encircle, perhaps, potato salad, chicken mayonnaise, or a soft cream cheese mixture. You can imagine the colour contrasts that may be achieved with this sort of presentation; much more attractive than displaying the food in glass dishes or silver on flats.

Individual moulded salads are produced in a similar manner, using dariole moulds or individual soufflé dishes with a smooth inside surface.

A few ideas for simple moulded salads are shown below. Firstly, a small selection of the many liquors you may care to use:

Tomato juice
Chicken or beef stock cube and water
Apple juice
Vegetable stock
Grapefruit juice
Grape juice
Lemon juice (bottled) and water or lime juice and water
Any creamed soup and water

When using bottled lime or lemon juices, add 1 dessertspoon of sugar to each $\frac{1}{2}$ pint (300ml) of water used. Do this when making any kind of savoury mould from bottled fruit juices which do not contain sugar. Use 2fl oz of the lime or lemon juice to $\frac{1}{2}$ pint (300ml) of water.

As you will appreciate, some of these liquors will give you a clear moulded salad, some a cloudy mould. It is obviously of little use taking the trouble to decorate (internally) a salad that is opaque, so if you are attempting a decorated salad use only clear stocks, apple juice or lime juice.

This list of suitable liquors in which to melt the gelatine will no doubt inspire you with ideas of the type of fillings that each would enhance. Of course, you will be aiming for flavour contrast between the gelatine mould and the more solid filling, and if the filling is a mixture of two or more foods, then you will be trying for texture contrast also. Here are a few ideas for fillings to match against your own choice of liquor:

Finely chopped celery, crushed pineapple and sweet corn
Grated raw carrot and finely-chopped watercress
Diced chicken and green peas
Macedoine of vegetables
Chopped celery, grated onion and cucumber dice
Chopped celery, green peppers and pimento
Cole-slaw (marinade, then drain and use)
Cole-slaw with diced potatoes
Grated carrot and cooked peas
Diced meat and assorted vegetables

Unmoulding Salads
Large moulds　Loosen the edge of the mould with a knife or spatula that has been dipped in hot water, after which the ring should leave the mould (if you have pre-dipped it in cold water before filling). If the ring does not

Opposite: Moulded ring salads (page 76–81)

come away, quickly immerse the mould in tepid water just up to the top. Dry the mould, so the drips will not fall on the service dish, then shake the mould to loosen. Moisten the surface of the gelatine ring and *also* the surface of the serving dish. The two wet surfaces will assist in making the jelly easy to place in the centre of the dish. Now place the serving dish on top of the mould, invert and lift the mould off carefully.

Small moulds   Individual moulds that will not come away from the gelatine ring after an initial loosening and a shake should be inverted in the hand and placed under running water as warm as the hand can comfortably stand. Do not let the gelatine come into contact with hot water.

Garnishing the Salad Ring

The garnish for a salad is just as important to its attractiveness as to any other food item, and the best position for such garnish is around the base of the ring itself. Keep the garnish simple; don't over-decorate. One important point to remember. Do not turn your moulded salad on to a serving dish that has been covered with lettuce leaves, for if the gelatine is tender (as it should be) the ribs of the lettuce may cut into the gelatine, and the ring could collapse! To my mind, the best sort of garnish for a gelatine salad is just simple bunches of crisp parsley or watercress or perhaps slices of cucumber around the base. If the garnish gets too fussy, the effect of the moulded salad is lost in confusion. So make the base garnish simple.

Fig. 124: Moulded salads – ring

Easy Moulded Fruit Salad

An easy way to produce moulded fruit salad is to rely upon the various degrees of 'porosity' of fruits, which make some of them float and others sink.

The floaters are slices or dice of fresh grapefruit, pear, banana, apple, strawberry. Nuts also float.

The sinkers are fresh grapes, orange slices, slices of canned apricots, pears, peaches, pineapple and cherries.

Ordinary jelly crystals or cubes are used to make fruit salads, although

Toast floats to complement different soups (page 86)

there are a number of occasions when a fruit juice may be more appropriate (such as on a 'diet' buffet).

The same rules for unmoulding this type of salad are followed, and the garnish should be such that it compliments the ring rather than distracts. I have found that a simple decoration of small bunches of green and black frosted grapes is one of the better surrounds for this type of salad.

SALAD DRESSINGS

Before we leave this chapter, a little should be said about salad dressings and mayonnaise. There are many types and kinds of dressings used for salads; both the type and the time when it is added can add considerably to the salad or ruin it completely.

With the exception of salads such as mixed salad using *canned vegetables* (which depend upon marination for flavour) the major rule is that the dressing should be added just before serving. Dressing has a tendency to wilt fresh salad greens, draw the juices from cucumber (and fruit) and cause protein salads to become watery. One should be sparing with the dressing for mixed or tossed salads. Use just enough to coat each leaf and make it sparkle and shine, so that there will be no excess in the bowl.

Below is a list of suitable dressings for specific types of salad:

Green lettuce, endive, chicory, watercress and so on require a plain French dressing or a variation of a French dressing.

Meat and fish salads require a heavy mayonnaise, sometimes spiced.

Potato, cabbage and egg salads call for a thin, spicy mayonnaise to bring out their best qualities.

Vegetable salads such as tomato, cucumber, asparagus, use a French dressing, a variation, or a thin, spicy mayonnaise.

French Dressing
Mix together a dash of salt and pepper and a little dry mustard and sugar. Add $\frac{1}{4}$ pint (150ml) wine vinegar and $\frac{1}{2}$ pint (300ml) salad oil.

Variations
Cheese To $\frac{3}{4}$ pint (450ml) of French dressing add 1oz (25g) crumbled Danish blue cheese

Chiffonade To $\frac{3}{4}$ pint (450ml) of French dressing add $\frac{1}{2}$ chopped hard-boiled egg, 1 teaspoon chopped green peppers and 1 teaspoon chopped red pimento

Chutney To $\frac{3}{4}$ pint (450ml) French dressing add 2oz (50g) chopped chutney

Curry To ¾ pint (450ml) of French dressing add 1 teaspoon curry powder

Horseradish To ¾ pint (450ml) of French dressing add 1 tablespoon horseradish cream

Mayonnaise Variations

Belvedere To 1 pint (600ml) mayonnaise, add 1 tablespoon tomato sauce, 2oz (50g) Danish blue cheese and 1 teaspoon chopped chives

Caviar To 1 pint (600ml) mayonnaise, add 1 teaspoon chopped onion, 1 tablespoon lemon juice, 2oz (50g) Danish caviar (lumpfish roe)

Cumberland To 1 pint (600ml) mayonnaise beat in 2oz (50g) currant jelly and finish with 1 tablespoon grated lemon rind

Herb Mayonnaise To 1 pint (600ml) of mayonnaise, add 2 teaspoons chopped parsley, 2 teaspoons chopped chives, ½ teaspoon oregano and 1 dessertspoon lemon juice

Sauce Verte Colour 1 pint (600ml) mayonnaise a light green with artificial food colouring and add 1 dessertspoon *each* of chopped capers, green olives and black olives

Tomato Mayonnaise To 1 pint (600ml) mayonnaise, add 1 dessertspoon of tomato paste and 2 teaspoons Worcestershire sauce

SOUPS

A few centuries ago, when ordinary people lived on soups and soupy stews, it was a point of pride to be able to say that a palatable soup could be made out of nothing. Indeed, the thriftier cooks often boasted, perhaps in self-defence, that even a simpleton could make a soup given a pot of water, a little salt and a few vegetables. This may indicate that, whilst times and diets have changed, simpletons have not. For whether making soup from simple or elaborate ingredients, even today it takes time, good taste, skill and care to prepare a delicious soup; it is no job for a simpleton.

In these modern times, of course, soup every day is not an arbitary requirement, and certainly not on a buffet. Furthermore, there are such excellent canned, packet and convenience soups on the market, in a variety to suit every taste, that there is no need to take time and trouble to produce soups from scratch.

The service of soup, too, is a matter of good taste, for on a buffet as with a more formal occasion, soup often sets the tone and quality of the food to follow. If the buffet is substantial, it is usually a kindness to select for the overture a light consommé, to arouse anticipation and whet the appetite without dulling it.

A hot, fragrant, full-flavoured consommé is perhaps the best compliment to your guests' discerning taste. An indifferent consommé is at best a waste of time and at worst, a positive affront. The great beauty of consommé is its crystal clarity. A garnish of some sort is therefore needed to emphasise and at the same time increase the enjoyment of the clear liquid. Try some of these ideas which give the soup a texture contrast.

Chicken Consommé
Toasted almonds; julienne carrots; garden peas; curried croûtons; garlic toast squares; sprig of fresh mint; sliced green olives; grated Parmesan; chopped parsley; watercress; bits of crisped bacon; thinly sliced orange; julienne of ham; slivers of avocado pear

Beef Consommé
Rounds of frankfurter sausage; garlic toast squares; chopped green peppers; sliced raw mushroom; grated Parmesan; diced red pimento; watercress; cucumber balls; chopped chive; radish slices

Clear Turtle
Chopped almonds; sliced lemon; diced pimento; chopped hard-boiled egg

In addition to these three basic consommés, there are a wide variety of cream soups available, a selection of which are shown in the following chart with appropriate garnishes cross-indexed.

	Almonds, toasted	Bacon, crispy bits	Carrots, julienne	Celery, sliced	Chiffonade	Cream, with dusting of nutmeg	Croûtons (thyme)	Cheese, grated	Frankfurter, rounds	Garlic toast, squares	Herbs, fresh, chopped	Green peppers, chopped	Ham, julienne	Lemon, thinly sliced	Mint	Olives, green, sliced	Olives, black, sliced	Orange, grated rind	Parmesan cheese	Cucumber, thinly sliced	Red pimento, diced
Asparagus		x	x			x			x					x	x		x			x	
Celery	x	x	x				x	x	x	x			x	x		x	x	x		x	x
Chicken	x		x		x							x				x	x	x	x	x	
Mushroom	x	x	x	x		x	x	x		x			x	x					x	x	x
Pea	x	x	x	x	x	x	x	x	x	x	x	x	x	x		x		x	x	x	x
Spinach		x	x				x	x			x			x							x
Tomato							x		x											x	
Watercress							x							x		x	x				

Flavourmates
For a new and exciting flavour, and to give your first course an individual touch, try amalgamating soups that are natural 'flavourmates' – soups that blend together beautifully and will provide contrasts to each other and, in so doing, produce an unusual but delightful taste experience. You may call each of these mixtures any name you wish, and in fact on special

occasions you may care to christen your own amalgamation after the principal guest or client. Some suggestions are shown on the list below – *all* are creamed soups. Amalgamate equal quantities of column 1 and column 2.

Blend	With	Garnish
Tomato	Mushroom	Sliced radish
Tomato	Chicken	Diced green peppers
Tomato	Beef Bouillon	Cooked spaghetti
Tomato	Milk	Chopped, skinned tomatoes
Tomato	Celery	Baked beans
Chicken	Celery	Julienne of celery
Chicken	Mushroom	Diced ham
Chicken	Green Pea	Croûtons
Celery	Beef Bouillon	Julienne of celery
Mushroom	Beef Bouillon	Diced, cooked liver

Soup Companions

There is no need to serve the usual plain bread, rolls or crackers with soup. Try something a little different. For example, garlic bread gives an interesting touch; Melba toast is more traditional.

Garlic Bread

Crush 1 clove of garlic with $\frac{1}{2}$ teaspoon of salt and cream in 2oz (50g) of butter. Slice a French loaf right along its length at $\frac{1}{2}$in (1cm) intervals, but without cutting right through the bottom crust. Spread the garlic-flavoured butter in between the slices. Should there be any remaining, spread this over the outside of the loaf. Now wrap the whole loaf in aluminium foil and place in a hot oven for 10 minutes. Serve while still warm.

Melba Toast

Cut white bread in $\frac{1}{4}$in (6mm) slices or use the 'thin-cut' sliced bread. Toast evenly on both sides, then remove the crusts with a sharp knife, split each piece of toast in two and return to the grill or salamander and toast the 'uncooked' side. Allow sufficient space between the heat source and the toast, as the bread will tend to curl during the second toasting.

Croûtons

Dice dry bread into pieces about $\frac{1}{4}$in (6mm) square and either sauté them in butter or brown them in a hot oven. It is sometimes an attractive idea to offer herb croûtons. Should you wish to do this, place the warm croûtons in a thick plastic bag with 1 teaspoon salt and some finely chopped herbs. The herbs may be chosen from parsley, thyme, basil or rosemary. Alternatively, the grated rind of orange or lemon may also be used, and of course, grated Parmesan cheese is a great favourite. Try also, minced onion or curry powder.

Toast Floats

A most attractive form of garnish on soup is pieces of toast cut into rounds with a metal cutter and decorated with various garnishes. They are prepared in advance, and just when the soup is being served, the floats are placed in the centre.

The toast floats should be cut about $\frac{1}{4}$in (6mm) thick and the diameter a little larger than a 10 penny coin.

Here are a few ideas.

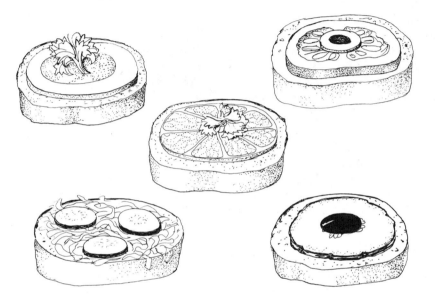

Fig. 125 : Toast floats

5

Sandwiches and Canapés

When sandwiches are required for an occasion, it is a good idea to include a few less common types to heighten the interest. Among the most acceptable in this category are pinwheel, ribbon, mosaic, draught-board and roll-ups. Although the type of bread you use will vary according to the type of sandwich, one constant factor in sandwich making is the *butter spread*.

The most important thing is that you should not be mean about the quantity of butter you use. A liberal spreading of butter makes the difference between a poor sandwich and one that is eaten with relish. At least ½lb (225g) should be used for every 20 rounds of 'conventional' sandwiches. Apart from butter used straight from the wrapper, 'savoury butters' will often add an additional and exciting flavour to the sandwich by giving it an unexpected contrast.

A savoury butter is made by the addition of certain ingredients to the softened butter. Here are a few suggestions:

Name	Method	Use
Anchovy	Use equal quantities of fillet of anchovy and butter. Add pepper and cayenne. Mix into a smooth spread	For both savouries and sandwiches
Caper	Chop 1 teaspoon capers very finely. Season with salt and pepper and mix with 2oz (50g) butter	Ideal with meat sandwiches, especially roast lamb
Cheese	1oz (25g) grated cheese to 2oz (50g) butter. Add a dash of mustard and a little pepper	Especially good with any type of fish filling
Chives	One dessertspoon chopped chives to 2oz (50g) butter. Add lemon juice, salt and pepper	For sandwiches with a cream cheese base

Name	Method	Use
Garlic	Crush ½ clove garlic and mix with 8oz (225g) softened butter	Suitable for any type of filling
Herb	Use any freshly chopped green herb, mix with a little lemon juice and blend with softened butter	Use with fish sandwiches
Lemon	Grated rind and zest of 1 lemon to 4oz (100g) creamed butter	Fish or sharp cheese sandwiches
Lobster coral	Mix coral well with the softened butter and season with salt and pepper	With fish or cream cheese
Mustard	½ teaspoon French mustard, blend with dash Worcestershire sauce in 4oz (100g) butter	For meat and especially ham sandwiches
Orange	Similar recipe to that for lemon butter	Pork, duck, ham sandwiches
Oregano	½ teaspoon oregano to 4oz (100g) butter	For ham, tongue or salami
Spice	¼ teaspoon cinnamon to 4oz (100g) butter	Cheese or liver pâté

Pinwheel Sandwiches

Use a loaf of day-old unsliced bread. Place the loaf on the cutting board and with a long, sharp knife, slice off all the crusts except the bottom one.

Next, with the crust-side of the loaf on your left-hand side, cut slices lengthways about ⅛in (3mm) to ¼in (6mm) thick. This may be done on a slicing machine. Now run a rolling pin over each slice, starting at the narrow end. This makes the bread easier to handle and less likely to crack when rolled.

Spread each slice with softened butter right to the edge, then cover with the chosen filling. A moist (creamed) filling is best. If desired, place three or more stuffed olives across the short end.

Starting at the end with the stuffed olives, tightly roll the slice, being careful to keep the sides in line. A tight roll makes slicing easier, and achieves neat pinwheels with distinctive markings.

Wrap rolls individually in waxed paper or foil, twisting the ends to keep out the air. Chill for several hours or overnight. Remove about 1 hour before they are required, and cut into slices about ½in (1cm) thick.

Lift with a palette knife on to serving dishes or trays. Cover with foil or a damp cloth and keep in refrigerator until needed (Fig. 126).

Ribbon Sandwiches

Using fresh bread, spread slices of wholemeal (or any brown bread) and

Opposite: Royal canapés (page 96–8)
Overleaf: Mosaic sandwiches (page 90–1)

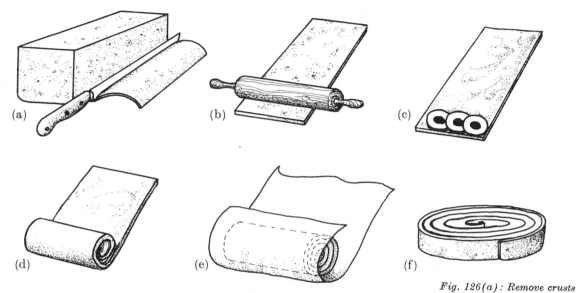

Fig. 126(a): Remove crusts
(b): Roll out bread slice
(c): Spread filling and
arrange olives
(d): Roll tightly
(e): Wrap rolls separately
(f): Finished pinwheel
sandwich

white bread with butter and desired filling – it must be moist – then stack alternately, white and brown.

Press together firmly each stack of slices. Then, with a sharp knife and using a 'sawing' motion, slice the crusts from sides of each stack.

Arrange stacks on a dish, cover with foil or waxed paper and chill for about 4 hours. Then cut into ½in (1cm) strips.

Cut each slice into thirds, halves or triangles. Arrange on a serving platter. Remember that the fillings must be moist to keep the slices joined (Fig.127).

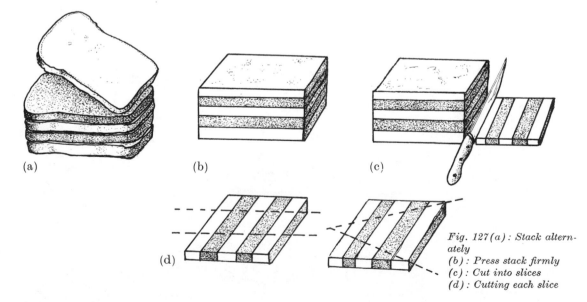

Fig. 127(a): Stack alternately
(b): Press stack firmly
(c): Cut into slices
(d): Cutting each slice

A *Opposite: Lobster Parisienne (page 103)*
B *Previous Page: Prawn chariots (page 105)*

Draughtboard Sandwiches

Use 2 slices of brown bread and two slices of white bread. Alternate them – brown, white, brown, white and butter and fill them as in steps 1 and 2 of the ribbon sandwich instructions.

Cut the stack into ½in (1cm) slices, then put three alternating slices together, so that a finger of white bread is next to a finger of brown bread both down and across, as shown here. Remember to use a good spread to make the sections stay together.

Chill for 4 hours. Remove from refrigerator and with a sharp knife *immediately* slice into draughtboard slices about ½in (1cm) thick. These sandwiches must be sliced while they are *really* cold (Fig. 128).

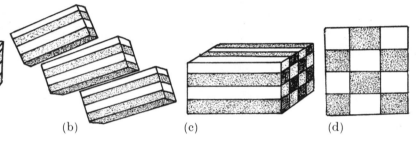

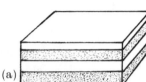

(a)

(b)   (c)   (d)

Fig. 128: (a): Stack alternately
(b): Cut into slices
(c): Slice when very cold
(d): Finished result

Mosaic Sandwiches

To make these interesting sandwiches, you use a normal size pastry cutter and a medium size aspic cutter to stamp the designs. Take a slice of white bread and a slice of brown bread and stamp out the shape with the pastry cutter. You will now have a circle of white bread and a circle of brown bread. Now, with the smaller cutter, stamp out the shape in the centre of both circles of bread, and remove the cut shape.

Then, alternate the base and mosaic insert, putting the brown 'insert'

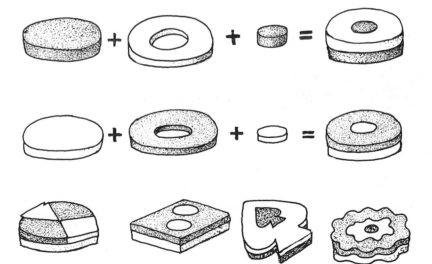

Fig. 129: Types of mosaic sandwiches

into the white bread circle, and the white 'insert' into the brown bread circle. This makes the top slice of the sandwich.

To complete the sandwich, place this top slice on a circle of bread, also cut with the pastry cutter, which has been spread with butter and a filling. Put the mosaic slice on top and the sandwich is complete.

The effect is more dramatic if you use the same type of bread for the base as for the mosaic. The illustration shows you how the sandwiches should look when completed (Fig. 129).

Envelopes

Cut the crusts from thin slices of bread. Spread to the edge with butter, then with filling. Fold as shown, then press the centre points firmly or fasten with a cocktail stick. Garnish with slices of stuffed olive or similar.

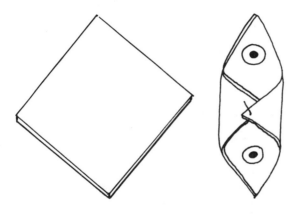

Fig. 130: Envelope sandwiches

Cornucopias

Trim the crusts from bread as above. Cut off corners from each slice. Spread slice with butter and filling. Roll as shown, with sides overlapping, and fasten with a cocktail stick. Put a strip of carrot or green pepper in the top.

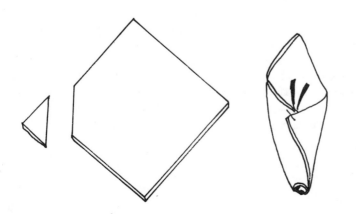

Fig. 131: Cornucopia sandwiches

The Sandwich Gâteau

One of the most interesting buffet items, and quite suitable for a 'place of honour' on any table, is the sandwich gâteau. It is simple to prepare and is really just a giant 'four-decker' sandwich coated with whipped cream cheese. It is a good idea to have each of the 'decks' filled with a different coloured spread, so that when the gâteau is cut the contrasts are very obvious. For example:

Red filling   4 slices of minced boiled ham with the addition of chopped pimento and moistened with a *very* little mayonnaise.
Green filling   Chopped gherkins and chopped watercress moistened with a *very* little mayonnaise.
Yellow filling   Mashed yolk of eggs (use three eggs) with a very little mayonnaise.
White filling   Cream cheese and chopped canned pineapple.
   The covering for the gâteau is made with three packets of cream cheese.

Fig. 132: Sandwich gâteau

Cut a quartern loaf lengthways, as for pinwheel sandwiches. Use five slices and butter them well. Mix each of your coloured fillings and bind them with sufficient mayonnaise so they will spread easily but will not ooze. Spread each filling on a separate slice, then stack them on top of each other. You spread four slices and use the fifth slice as the lid or top.

   Be sure not to press the gâteau too heavily while stacking. Scrape off any surplus filling with a knife, wrap the gâteau in foil, put in the refrigerator and chill well.

   Remove from the refrigerator then mix the cream cheese together with a little light cream. Beat well to make it easy to spread, then cover the entire gâteau (top and sides) with the cheese 'icing'. Garnish with slices of radish, stuffed olive, or as you wish. Return to the refrigerator until a few minutes prior to serving. Cut into slices with a sharp knife.

OPEN SANDWICHES

The popularity of open sandwiches is steadily increasing, and for very good reason. They look a dozen times better than the conventional sandwich with a filling between two pieces of bread. Of course they take longer to prepare, yet providing a little time is spent in pre-preparation, the simple examples shown below can be made surprisingly quickly. Of course, these do not have the elegance of the traditional Danish Smorrebrod, but they are inexpensive to prepare and very effective and decorative.

This type of open sandwich is based upon:

a) the bread
b) a creamed (or naturally soft) base
c) a main ingredient (contrasting item), which is meant to catch the eye
d) a garnish

The bread for these open sandwiches should be slices cut at an angle from a French baton or long loaf, so that each piece is of a size easily picked up from the service tray. The slices have to be of a manageable size. They should be cut just under ½ in (1 cm) – thick not so thin that they bend or sag as soon as they are picked up. Crusts should be left on the bread slices to provide extra stability, and the slices spread with butter.

Creamed bases may be made from almost any savoury item you care to use, minced or very finely chopped and then mixed with *just* sufficient mayonnaise to bind the ingredient and make a 'spreadable' mixture. A naturally soft base such as cream or cottage cheese is beaten until smooth and then extended if necessary with a little thin cream. Instead of using plain mayonnaise as the binding agent, you can try a mixture of mayonnaise and a flavoured aspic. Plain yogurt used as a binding agent or as an extender for cottage cheese is very good. Concentrated cream soups (the canned variety) may also be used straight from the can, in which case the base ingredient should be as bland as possible – finely chopped celery, chopped raw mushrooms, minced chicken. Do not use chopped ham, corned beef, tongue or any strong flavoured item.

The creamed base is spread on the oval slices of buttered bread with a spatula or wide-bladed knife to a thickness which will allow the main food item and the garnish to be 'anchored' in position, and not slide off when the slice is lifted.

Remember that by using a savoury butter, instead of a plain butter spread, an even greater permutation of flavours can be produced. But experiment carefully before you try to combine too many flavours.

On page 94 are just a few suggestions for these easy-to-make open sandwiches. The binding agent in most of these suggestions is mayonnaise, but as explained there are a number of alternatives you can try.

Fig. 133: Simple open sandwiches

Base	Main ingredient	Garnish
Grated hard cheese } with mayonnaise	Whole sardine Sprinkled chopped ham Sliced hard-boiled egg	$2 \times \frac{1}{2}$ tomato slice 2 cucumber slices Watercress sprigs
Soft cream cheese } with cream or yogurt	Crushed pineapple Chopped walnuts Diced beef	Chopped chives Watercress sprigs Radish slices
Chopped chicken } with mayonnaise	Shelled prawns	Lemon twist
Mashed liver sausage } with mayonnaise	Crisp bacon bits	Tomato slices
Chopped ham and mayonnaise	Sliced raw mushrooms	Green pepper strip
Chopped hard-boiled } egg and mayonnaise	Diced chicken/pimento Thinly-sliced salami 2 anchovy fillets, crossed	Lemon twist Strips red pimento Sliced stuffed olive in each quarter

When using Danish blue cheese as a base, it should first be blended with cottage cheese in the proportions of 4oz (100g) blue cheese to 12oz (325g) cottage cheese.

Any cold white fish, free of skin and bones may be used as a base; mix with a little anchovy paste before adding the mayonnaise.

SAVOURY CANAPÉS

There is probably nothing more showy than a tray of dainty canapés, cut in various shapes and tastefully decorated. On the face of it, these delicate pieces may seem to present great difficulty to prepare, and covering them with aspic when necessary is regarded as a time-consuming chore. However, there are two very quick and easy methods by which the most delicate canapés can be made and the instructions and methods of preparation are given below.

The first thing to remember is that canapés must be tender and slightly moist. Nothing is worse than a tough canapé made from rubbery toast, or a sloppy morsel that takes a great deal of manipulation to transport to one's mouth. The thickness of the bread base decides to a great extent whether the canapé will be tough or otherwise. Thin bread that has been toasted on both sides and then allowed to absorb moisture from the topping will undoubtedly become tough. Therefore, in the first place, see that the bread you use is about $\frac{1}{4}$in (6mm) thick : anything thinner will not be satisfactory. Secondly, in order that the toast shall remain crisp and dry (but not tough), be sure that the butter or the savoury spread used fully covers the toast base, right up to the edges.

There are two types of canapés – the royal canapé, which is produced for special occasions, and the 'standard' canapé, which is more often seen on buffet tables. The main difference between the two types is that the royal has a thin layer of scrambled egg spread over the buttered toast base. This gives the canapé a delightful softness of texture. Furthermore, 'royal' canapés are *always* glazed with aspic jelly. The 'standard' canapé does not have the egg spread over the base, and the bread is often toasted on one side only.

Standard Canapés

These are much easier and much quicker to prepare, and in many kitchens are produced by a very junior member of the kitchen staff. Below are the instructions and the total ingredients required to make 100 standard canapés in a very short time, and providing 8 varieties.

Purchasing list
$3\frac{1}{2}$lb (1·65 kg) loaf sliced laterally
$\frac{1}{2}$ pint (300ml) mayonnaise
3oz (75g) block of cream cheese
1 small can anchovies
$\frac{1}{2}$ teaspoon celery salt
1oz (25g) can red pimentos
3oz (75g) can chicken spread (or equivalent)
8ozs (225g) butter
3 stuffed olives
1 small can red salmon
$3\frac{3}{4}$oz (95g) can sardines in oil
1 lemon
4oz (100g) liver sausage
14 white cocktail onions
3oz (75g) salami, sliced very thinly
$\frac{1}{4}$ cucumber
3oz (75g) can ham (or meat) spread
1oz (25g) green pepper
1 egg, hard-boiled and sliced

Procedure
1 Lightly toast the sliced bread on one side. Turn the untoasted side (upon which the spreads are placed) upwards.

2 Trim off the crust to make a clean edge.

3 Lightly butter the untoasted side of each slice.

4 Mix 1½oz (40g) of cream cheese with ½oz (15g) anchovy paste. Spread on one slice of toast. Open the can of anchovies, cut each fillet into strips. Cut the toast into 12 fingers and decorate each finger with a small strip of anchovy.

5 Mix 2oz (50g) of cream cheese with the celery salt. Spread on one slice of the base. Decorate with a little of the pimento cut into strips or diamonds. Cut the toast into 12 fingers.

6 Open the can of chicken spread and moisten with a little mayonnaise. Spread on one slice of base. Garnish with half slices of hard-boiled egg. Cut the toast into 14 strips.

7 Drain the canned salmon and mix with a little mayonnaise. Spread on one slice of toast base and garnish with the red pimento cut into strips. Cut into 12 fingers.

8 Open the can of sardines, drain them and mash with a little mayonnaise. Spread mixture on a toasted base. Cut base into 12 finger strips. Cut the lemon into 6 thin slices, then cut each slice in half. Place a half-slice on each canapé.

9 Mix the mashed liver sausage with mayonnaise. Spread mixture on a toast base, then cut base into 14 strips. Garnish each strip with a white cocktail onion.

10 Cover a toast base with the thinly-sliced salami. Trim off any meat hanging over the side. Cut the toast into 12 strips and garnish with a thin cucumber slice.

11 Mix the can of ham spread with a little mustard and mayonnaise. Spread on the last piece of toast base, cut into 12 strips and garnish with a small piece of green pepper.

Of course, it is quite a simple matter to produce different shaped canapés by using fancy cutters, but in this case use only soft spreads on the toast base. If you try to cut through salami, ham or any hard meats, the cut will be ragged, and you may in fact find it almost impossible to produce a neat professional shape. Square or triangular canapés are simple to make by cutting the whole toast base into three equal sections, then cutting again to make the smaller squares, or from corner to corner to produce triangles.

'Royal' Canapés

1 Cut a 3½lb (1·65kg) loaf lengthways in slices no less than ¼in (6mm) thick. This will give you up to 12 slices of bread, and it is possible to produce 10 or more canapés from one slice.

2 Toast the sliced bread *lightly* on both sides, and gently press them flat while still warm. Do *not* stack the slices one on the other, or the toast will toughen.

3 Prepare a soft, tender and lightly-seasoned scrambled egg. It is most important that the egg is not cooked hard.

4 Butter the toasted bread and spread a thin layer of egg over each slice.

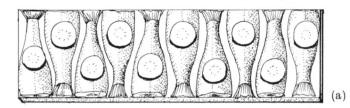

(a)

*Fig. 134(a) : Sardine
canapé
(b) : Frankfurter canapé
(c) : Shrimp canapé
(d) : Liver sausage canapé
(e) : Asparagus canapé
(f) : Tongue or ham canapé*

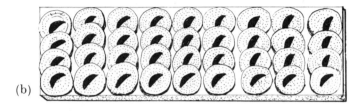

(b)

(c)

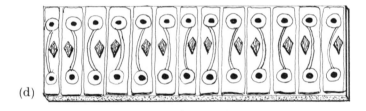

(d)

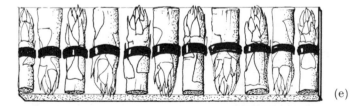

(e)

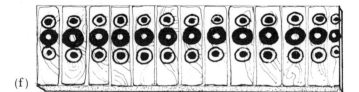

(f)

5 Have your toppings ready. In most cases 6 varieties will be sufficient. Let us suppose the following have been chosen – sardine; frankfurter; shrimp; liver sausage; asparagus tips and tongue.

Prepare these ingredients by draining the sardines and the asparagus tips, cutting the sauage, frankfurters and tongue into the desired shapes. Have your garnishes ready for the toppings – sliced, stuffed olives, black olives, sliced gherkins, radish, etc.

6 Take your first slice of toast which has been covered with scrambled egg and place the drained sardines in a row, alternating head and tail as shown in Fig. 134(a). Put the fish quite close together, allowing just enough room for a knife to cut between them. Garnish as desired.

Now proceed with the frankfurters. Take the sliced rounds and place three or four in a line on your second piece of toast, so that the slices are wedged in the egg base.

The third toast base is finished with shrimp, and again you will need 3 or 4 in a line. In between the fish you may like to place a slice of stuffed olive or radish to give a contrast. Keep the lines of shrimp distinct and separate, just allowing room for the knife to cut the canapé without disturbing the topping.

The liver sausage has been cut into 'baton' just a little shorter in length than the toast base, and about $\frac{3}{4}$in (2cm) wide. Place them in position on the fourth piece of toast. Garnish as desired.

Place the asparagus tips for toast No. 5 head to tail, alternating in a similar manner to that of the sardines. Then garnish as desired.

Cut the tongue (or ham if you prefer) to the same size as the liver sausage, and place the slices on toast No. 6 in a line as before. Garnish as desired.

When the toasts have been prepared, coat them lightly with aspic jelly.

To make aspic jelly (1 pint, 600ml)
$\frac{1}{2}$oz (12g) leaf gelatine
$\frac{3}{4}$ pint (450ml) meat stock or bouillon cube
1fl oz dry sherry
lemon juice
Soak gelatine in a little water. Add the hot stock together with the remaining ingredients and stir until dissolved. Chill and use as required.

Emergency Canapés

There are times, mercifully few in number, when the cook is asked to produce canapés in a very great hurry. When a considerable number are needed at short notice, I have found that the only way to produce, say, 300 canapés in under an hour is to cheat like mad! Like this:

The canapé base is made from quartern loaves of sandwich bread. The crusts are cut from the loaf, which is then sliced lengthways, into five long slices. Each slice is toasted on one side only.

The spreading mixture is made in a somewhat similar manner to those

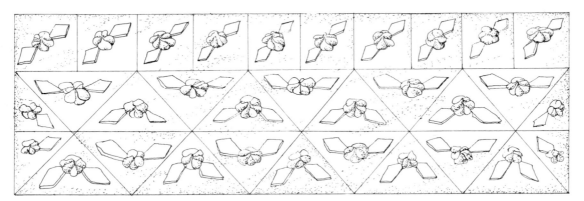

Fig. 135: Emergency canapés

used for open sandwiches, but using any 'soft' canned meats, such as corned beef, ham roll, turkey roll, etc. – anything to save time. If you have time to spare, then of course these restrictions need not apply. Liver sausage or any type of meat or fish pâté is also quite excellent as a savoury base, and cold white fish, prepared as it is for open sandwiches, may also be used. When mashed or beaten until soft, these ingredients are then mixed with softened butter and beaten until creamy and as smooth as possible. Use just enough butter to make the mixture creamy and easily spreadable. The toasted bread is then spread with the mixtures on the plain (untoasted) side. The toasted side forms the bottom of the canapés. Each slice is now cut *lengthways* into three, each slice giving 3 strips.

Each strip will cut into 10 bite-sized canapés, and each one is finished off with a decoration of stiffened mayonnaise piped with a small rose tube, and a suitable garnish.

Order of Preparation

1 Prepare ½ pint (300ml) of mild flavoured aspic (or unflavoured gelatine) and combine with 2 pints (1·25 litres) of mayonnaise. You may care to divide the mayonnaise and colour each part with vegetable colouring, tomato paste, anchovy paste, mushroom ketchup and so on.
2 Remove crusts from 2 sandwich loaves (large size), slice each lengthways into 5 slices and toast on one side.
3 Prepare meat and fish bases as described, and mix with the softened butter. Beat well.
4 Cut appropriate garnishes – tiny lemon pieces, sliced stuffed olives, watercress and parsley sprigs, green pepper and red pimento strips and diamonds, salted almonds, half walnuts, etc.
5 Cover toasts with creamed bases, cut each toast into 3 strips lengthways. You may now either pipe the decoration on each strip before cutting into the 10 individual pieces, or cut and pipe them afterwards. Whenever you decide to cut, do remember to vary the shapes. With the strips you may produce squares, triangles and diamond shapes without any of the strip being wasted.
6 After cutting, place garnish in position. Place on service tray and put in refrigerator.

6

Fish, Meat and Poultry

Decorative Salmon

Decorated whole salmon as a centre-piece lends luxury to the occasion. The fish can be presented in one of two ways – either laying on its side or on its belly.

Side Presentation

If the decoration is to be on one side of the fish, it is first of all cleaned, and the tail trimmed to a neat shape, following the contour of the natural tail. Poach the fish in a 'fumet' to which a little vinegar has been added. Place the fish in the cold liquor, then bring it to the boil and *simmer* until cooked. Allow 3 minutes per 1lb (450g) for fish weighing up to 8lb (3·6kg) $2\frac{1}{2}$ minutes for fish weighing up to 14lb (5·6kg) and 2 minutes per lb for fish over 14lb (5·6 kg). Let the salmon cool in its cooking liquor, then remove and place it on a rack to drain thoroughly.

When the fish is dry, put it on a decorative platter, and remove enough skin to show a reasonable area of flesh. The area to be decorated may be fairly small, or can run the length of the fish: it is a matter of personal preference. The shape of the area to be decorated may vary, too; it may be oval, diamond or rectangular. Smooth the flesh with the back of a knife.

After the skin has been removed, the fish should be thoroughly cooled in the refrigerator, then given a thick coat of aspic jelly. The various items of decoration should then be dipped in aspic and placed in position, and the whole decorated area glazed once more with aspic. Some cooks prefer to cover the area to be decorated with a fish mayonnaise prior to decoration and this is quite acceptable as a professional presentation.

Alternative Presentation

If the salmon is to be presented on its belly, then it must be cooked in a similar position so that it will maintain this natural appearance, and the flesh will remain intact after cooking. It is most often necessary to wrap the fish in a clean cloth around the body and tie with string. (The cloth is

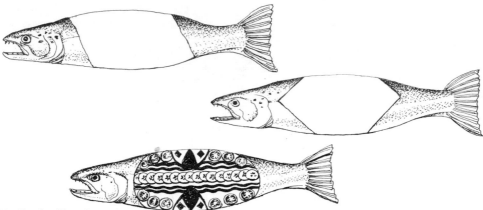

Fig. 136: Partly-skinned salmon

needed so the string will not cut into the delicate flesh and spoil its appearance.) The fish is then placed on the rack of the fish kettle and gently cooked. After cooking and cooling, the skin is removed from both sides of the salmon, the centre fin is also taken away and the fish is decorated in the manner desired, after covering the exposed surface with a mayonnaise *colée*.

From both a practical and an economic point of view it is often a good idea to produce a 'mock' salmon presentation, by making a fish *shape* with Russian salad or potato salad, and using the fish, with the exception of the head and part of the tail, as 'service portions'. This idea also saves considerable time by not having to cut salmon portions from the whole fish, in front of the guests.

To produce this presentation it is necessary to take the head of the salmon and about 6in (15cm) of the tail flesh and including the tail. The shape of the salmon, excluding the two pieces just mentioned, is formed by vegetable salad, chilled in the refrigerator, then covered with *chaudfroid* or mayonnaise *colée*. The head and the tail piece are then placed in position, and as far as the guests are concerned they are seeing a decorated whole salmon.

The two sides of the salmon are then made into fillets, decorated as required and placed on the platter around the 'mock' fish.

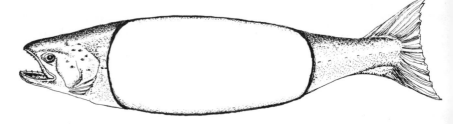

Fig. 137: 'Mock' salmon presentation

Medallions of Salmon
A convenient and economical method of producing individual portions of

salmon is by making medallions. The two sides of the salmon are removed to within 6in (15cm) of the tail. This section is left whole, with the skin intact. Remove skin and bones from the two fillets and cut into 2oz (50g) slices. Roll these fillets into round shapes and tie with thin string so they will keep their shape when cooking. Poach in a fish *fumet* for about 10 minutes and allow them to cool in the liquor, until quite cold. Remove from kettle and drain well. Place on a wire rack and pipe with a little mayonnaise *colée* to mask the top and present a smooth surface, then decorate as required. Remove string, then glaze each medallion with fish aspic. Arrange on the platter around the 'mock' salmon.

Lobster

Lobster in whatever form it is served is one of the most delicious foods that can be offered. Many attractive presentations have been evolved over the years, the two most popular being the 'Bellevue' and the 'Parisienne' styles. Below we show a simplified method of producing both these styles. It is not the classical method, but is fast and attractive.

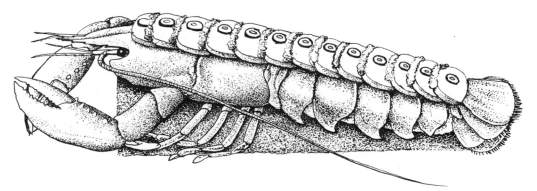

Fig. 138: Lobster Parisienne

Lobster Parisienne

Tie the lobster to a board with its tail straight out and cook in a well-salted fish *fumet* for the appropriate time. Allow to cool in its own liquor, then remove and wipe clean. Lay the lobster on its back on the table and with scissors cut a strip about 1in (2·5cm) wide, commencing at a point 1½in (4cm) from the tail end to the point where the tail meets the head. Cut carefully so that the shell does not break, then remove tail meat.

Cut the flesh into neat slices following the marks made by the shell, and dice the small amount of trimmings from the flesh. Fill the cavity made by the removal of the tail flesh with either vegetable salad or potato salad stiffened with a little aspic. Place in refrigerator to set. Mask each of the slices (scallops) with mayonnaise *colée*, allow to set, then decorate with tiny pieces of black olive, radish, egg white, etc. before glazing with a fish aspic.

The lobster shell is placed on a triangular display pedestal prepared in the following manner. Remove the crusts from a stale quartern loaf and cut it across from corner to corner. This will produce two triangular pieces of bread. Now, *either* spread both sides and the top of the triangle with margarine or butter and sprinkle chopped parsley thickly all over to make an attractive green pedestal *or* put the triangle in very hot fat in the deep-fryer and cook until golden. Allow to cool, then brush the bottom with egg white, and place in a pre-heated platter. The egg will coagulate and keep the display pedestal firmly in position.

Put the lobster on the pedestal and secure it by cocktail sticks. Pipe mayonnaise *colée* down the centre of the lobster and set the decorated sliced tail meat at equal intervals along the length of the shell. Mix the body meat and the claw meat and any flesh trimmings with a little mayonnaise *colée* (just enough to moisten) and spoon this mixture between the slices of tail meat. Surround the platter with stuffed eggs, vegetables in aspic and small tomato lilies stuffed with shrimp.

Lobster Bellevue

The cooked lobster is split in half. The thin intestinal vein that runs down the centre of the tail is removed, as also is the stomach sac, the green liver and the gills at the sides of the body.

A good vegetable salad moistened with mayonnaise is filled into the head part of the shell, and pieces from the cracked claws are chopped and placed on top of the salad. The tail meat is cut into four sections; the meat from the left-hand slices are placed in the right-hand shell and vice versa. The lobster meat is decorated with tiny pieces of truffle aspic.

Crab

There are very few ways that crab can be served on a buffet, the most well-known style being 'dressed crab'. To dress a crab is a time-consuming chore and one which in my opinion is hardly worth the effort. The crab meat itself is often used for crab salad and other simple dishes, but if this is the requirement it is much more practical to purchase crab meat in a packet.

Crayfish

These delicate shellfish are a fresh-water variety and because of their subtle flavour must always be prepared from the live state. A fish *fumet* or *court bouillon* is prepared in which the fish are cooked for 10 minutes.

But first the fish must be eviscerated by removing the intestine that runs through the body. To do this, find the centre tail fin (you will notice that there are five little fins in the tail), pull out the central one and the intestines will come away with it.

As soon as this is done, the crayfish should be cooked without delay. After cooking, allow the fish to cool in the liquor. Then carefully crack and remove the tail shells, but keep the cooked meat retained in the body of the fish.

Crayfish may be used to great decorative effect in a 'horse and cart' presentation in the following manner. Cut a grapefruit in half, cut away the flesh (to use another time) and serate the cut edge of the shell. Fill the

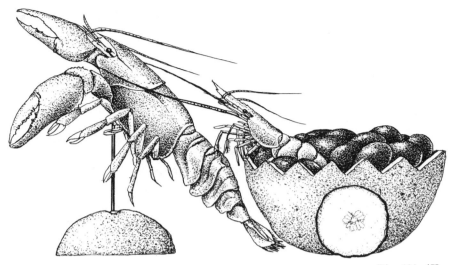

Fig. 139: 'Horse and cart' using crayfish

shell with appetisers such as olives or a fish dip. Cut 2 slices of cucumber for the wheels. Place a whole prawn as the 'driver', and a crayfish as the 'horse'. Support the fish on a cocktail stick stuck into a half lemon, as shown.

Crawfish

Sometimes called Cape Lobster because of the large quantities brought over to this country in the 1940s and 1950s, these sea-water shellfish resemble the lobster, except that they do not have claws. Crawfish may be used and decorated in a similar manner to lobster. However, if it is to be prepared in the 'Parisienne' style, remove the shell from the top to reach the tail meat, not from underneath the fish as with lobster.

Prawns

These are an economical shellfish. In their uncooked state they are between 2 and 4in (5 and 10cm) long, grey and almost transparent. When they are cooked, they turn a bright pink. It is most important not to overcook them – a maximum of 5 minutes in boiling salted water is sufficient. Most of the prawns used today are bought shelled and pre-packed.

Prawns make an excellent decorative piece when peeled and stuck on cocktail sticks and speared on to a grapefruit or a hollowed cabbage.

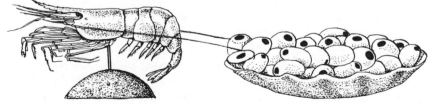

Fig. 140: Prawn 'chariot'

Fresh prawns with their shells intact can also become part of a decorative centre-piece. Put a cocktail stick through a prawn and stick the other end in a half-lemon (as with the crayfish presentation). Place a number of these on a tray and have pastry barquettes or other small food containers being pulled along by the prawns.

Shrimps

These tiny shellfish were found in enormous quantities around the coast of Britain, but recent overfishing has depleted the stock to an alarming extent. Consequently most shrimp are now imported, ready shelled and ready cooked. Raw shrimp are pale grey with a greenish tinge and semi-transparent, but after cooking in boiling salted water for 4 minutes, they take on their traditional reddish colour.

Apart from using shrimp in salads and as individual decorative items on larger presentations, the most popular method of serving them is as 'potted shrimp'. These are prepared by melting 8oz (225g) butter to each 8oz (225g) of fish in a saucepan, adding a pinch of ground mace, a little cayenne pepper and a dash of nutmeg. Add the fish and heat thoroughly and *very* gently until the fish is impregnated with the flavour of the spices, but on no account let the mixture boil. When ready, pour the mixture into individual pots and seal each with equal quantities of clarified butter.

DECORATIVE MEATS

Almost every type of meat and poultry lends itself to decorative treatment, and in this section we show ideas which you may like to try.

Standing Rib of Beef

There is something very striking about having a cold standing roast on the buffet table, and it should be prepared in the following manner for the best results. Remove the excess fat and roast the meat until it is fairly well done. If it is too rare, not only will it look unappetising when sliced, but the juices will run and stain the platter. When cold, trim the joint again but do not cut the outer crisp cover, just any tiny pieces that may spoil the appearance. Now cut the whole joint in half down the centre, cut one half of the meat from the bone, and thinly slice it. The slices should be neatly displayed around the base of the 'display joint'. This other half is trimmed of the flank meat so that the joint presents a neat and compact appearance, the bones showing perhaps 2in (5cm) above the meat. Place a bread base under the presentation roast to catch any juice that may drip. Dress the exposed bones with ham ruffs. Fill in any exposed part of the platter, and the corners, with stuffed tomatoes, bunches of parsley and similar decoration. Slices of meat that are left after service may be returned to the kitchen to be made into cornets: rolled and glazed slices and *chaudfroid:*

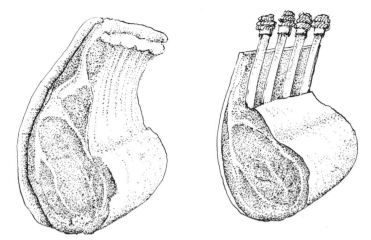

Fig. 141: Decorated stand-ing roast

Lamb

Two popular presentations are crown roast of lamb and decorated saddle of lamb. This is how they are prepared.

Crown Roast

Made from a pair of best-ends. The chine bones are removed and the rather dry skin from the back is stripped off. Care must be taken to see that the external covering of fat is not cut or taken off with this skin. The ribs are separated by knife cuts from the inside of the joints, but allowing the skin which holds the bones to remain in one piece. Thus, the joints will be suffic-iently supple to bend into the shape of a crown. Join the two best-ends together by passing string through the last rib and tying. Then repeat on the other side so that the crown is formed. The rib ends are cut away to about 1in (2·5cm) from the top and after the joint has been cooked and any final trimming completed, the bone ends are covered with cutlet frills. Often the cavity in the centre of the crown roast is filled with forcemeat, or may be filled with shredded lettuce after cooking. The piece is brought to the table whole and each portion is served by cutting between the rib bones and through the skin that holds them together.

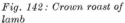

Fig. 142: Crown roast of lamb

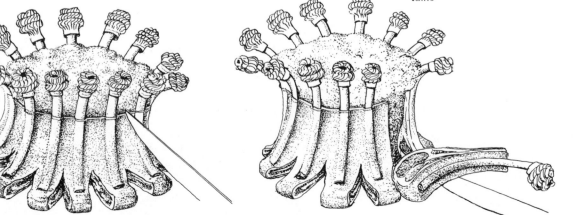

Fig. 143: Decorated saddle

Decorated Saddle

A saddle of lamb is a double loin and is a very impressive roast when brought to the carving table whole. To prepare it, first remove the hard skin as explained earlier by scoring down the backbone and skinning at an angle from belly to back and from head to tail. Wrap the tail in foil to protect it while cooking. Roast for 20 minutes to each pound (450g). Allow the joint to cool, then remove the belly flaps. Cut the meat away from the backbone from *under* the joint, working from the rib bones towards the backbone, but leaving a little skin over the top of the backbone so that the two loins remain whole. Glaze lightly with a little aspic and decorate as desired. Slices are cut across the joint on either side of the backbone.

Lamb Cutlets

There are a number of ways that lamb cutlets may be made an attractive addition to your presentation and opposite are a few you may care to try.

Trimming the cutlet   Trim ¾in (18mm) of meat to expose the bone. This is a basic preparation and all cutlets should be treated in this manner.

The trimmed cutlets should be pan-fried in clarified butter, then set to cool under a little pressure. (Lay them flat and place a baking tray over them.) This will give the cutlets a flat surface upon which the decoration may be placed. When quite cold, coat with *chaudfroid*, decorate and glaze.

Fig. 144: Trimming the cutlet. (a): Whole cutlet; (b): with meat trimmed from bone

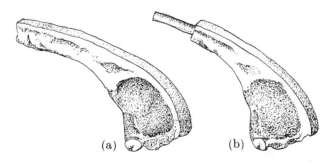

(a)   (b)

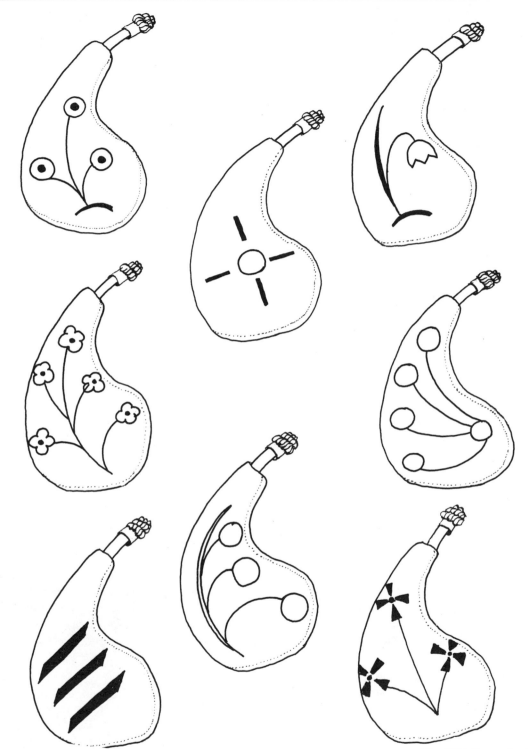

Fig. 145: Decorative ideas for lamb cutlets

Pork

Pork fillet and pork loin are most often seen as decorative pieces.

Pork Fillet

The fillet is gently roasted then sliced obliquely so that almost oval-shaped pieces of meat are obtained. The slices are then trimmed, covered with *chaudfroid*, decorated and glazed.

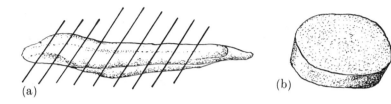

Fig. 146: Pork fillet.
(a): Sliced obliquely;
(b): resulting medallion

(a)   (b)

Pork Loin

Pork loin is firstly boned, sliced into cutlets ½in (1cm) thick, pan-fried and when cold trimmed to shape. They are then covered with *chaudfroid* and decorated. After the decorations are in place the cutlets are put into a dish containing cooled aspic. When the aspic is set, the cutlets are cut out with a sharp knife.

Roast Suckling Pig

For a presentation in the grand manner there is little that can beat a small roast suckling pig. This is how it is prepared.

Obtain a scalded pig from the butcher. Score the skin in the usual way, using oblique strokes (an angle of about 45 degrees is about right) working from head to tail. Prepare a stuffing of sage, onions and breadcrumbs in the usual manner, but add about 5 per cent butter (by weight) to the mixture. Moisten with a little milk if necessary. Stuff the piglet and sew up the opening with thread. Open the mouth and put an orange in it, keeping it in place with a cocktail stick. Tuck the legs underneath and put the pig on a wire rack in a roasting pan with a little water in it. Brush the pig well with egg white. Cook at 350°F (190°C), allowing about 15 minutes to each pound (450g). When the ears and nose are brown, cover them with foil to prevent burning. Serve on a large dish on a bed of watercress. Put a fresh orange in the mouth and a small flower (a daisy, for example) in each eye socket.

Ham

Ham is perhaps the most popular item on a buffet, and although it may appear difficult to prepare and decorate, this is not the case, as the following instructions will show.

Soak the ham in cold water for 24 hours, then scrub off the 'bloom' in warm water. Bring to the boil in fresh cold water and simmer very gently at 185°F (90°C) for the required period, allowing 20 minutes to each pound (450g) and 30 minutes extra. Allow the ham to cool in the cooking liquor, then remove it and while it is still warm, take off the skin. When quite cold, trim the ham as shown in Fig. 147(b).

To decorate, place the ham on a wire tray over a pan. Coat the entire area with *chaudfroid* sauce and let it cool. Prepare your decorations both for the ham itself and for any border design you may wish to put on the display tray. Dip the decorations for the ham in cooling aspic and place them in position. When all the decorations are set, coat them with a thin film of aspic and keep cool until required for service.

You may wish to decorate the ham with a bouquet of assorted flowers and leaves or some other quite difficult and time-consuming theme, but for speed and simplicity you may care to try the following idea. Select three perfect whole tinned pimentos, trim off the ragged edges, then fold back the top 'petals' of each so that they resemble Flanders poppies. Put ½ teaspoon of chopped black olives in the centre of each bloom. Cut foliage stems from cucumber rinds. Arrange the three poppies in the centre of the ham, towards the front. Put stems in position, and cover the entire decoration with a thin film of aspic. A good effect is obtained by leaving a serrated collar of ham skin at the top of the centre-piece, rather than removing all the skin and covering the entire ham section with *chaudfroid*.

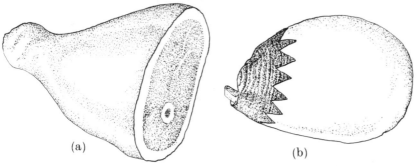

(a)

(b)

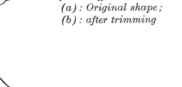

Fig. 147: Preparing ham for a buffet.
(a): Original shape;
(b): after trimming

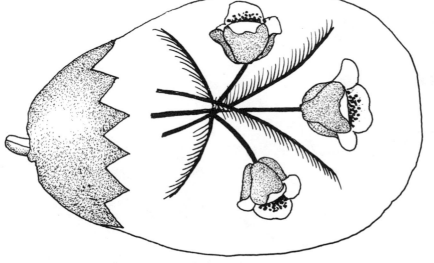

Fig. 148: Simple decorated ham

Fig. 149: Design ideas for chicken

Opposite: Lamb cutlets in chaudfroid (page 108–9)

POULTRY

Poultry has always been a great favourite on the menu and has the advantage of lending itself to many forms of decorative treatment.

Whole Chicken
To decorate whole chicken for the centre-piece, first poach the bird in a rich white stock, and allow to cool in the liquor. Remove the skin and cut out the breast with the bones. Coat the thighs and sides of the chicken with cooling *chaudfroid* sauce and allow to set. Cut the two breasts into 10 slices, trim and cover with *chaudfroid*, then decorate as desired. Now glaze with aspic.

The traditional method of filling and decorating the bird is to prepare some liver pâté mixed with a little creamed butter and fill the empty cavity of the chicken with this mixture, shaping it into the form of a breas⁺. It is then covered with *chaudfroid*, decorated as required and glazed with a thin film of aspic.

An economical filling for the breast, instead of using pâté, is well-beaten mashed potato. It is just as simple to make into a smooth surface and cover with *chaudfroid* in the usual way. This will not get you a prize at Hotelympia, but it works! A few design ideas are shown below:

Breast of Chicken
Small *chaudfroids* of chicken are produced from the breast meat. They are cut into finger-sized lengths and trimmed to the same shape – oval at one end and pointed at the other. This shape can be obtained by using an appropriate cutter. For a truly professional finish a small quantity of liver paste moistened with cream is placed on top of each breast to make a small mound. The medallions are then placed on a wire rack, cooled in the refrigerator and covered with *chaudfroid* sauce. After cool it again, each piece is decorated, then glazed.

Turkey
Turkey is treated in a similar manner to chicken. The bird is, however, always roasted (not poached) and the breast meat is cut into a considerably larger number of portions, as it is sliced rather than cut into finger-sized ovals. Breast of turkey is not often decorated, the slices being displayed on a dish around the decorated bird.

Opposite: A whole ham in chaudfroid (page 111)

7

Decorative Desserts

Very often we find that while considerable care and imagination has been given to the earlier courses in a buffet, the dessert section falls way behind in decorative appeal. As a result the last course, instead of finishing the meal in a grand style, serves only as an anti-climax. Of course, the type of desserts that are both practical and suitable for service on a buffet are somewhat limited, but there is no reason at all why whatever *is* presented should not have a certain flair.

Some of the most interesting and decorative desserts are made from various types of pastry, and although it is easy to buy ready-cooked tart shells and flan cases, if there is time to spare a far better product is obtained from a home-baked pastry. In order to get the best results it is necessary that the paste is of a quality and *texture* most suitable for the purpose for which it will be used. So although the number of recipes given in this book has been kept to the minimum, it might be appropriate to include just three pastry recipes which will add tremendously to the enjoyment of the dessert of which they are a part.

Pâte à Foncée
This rich shortcrust is generally used for tarts and flans that are to be eaten cold.

2lb (900g) plain flour	just over $\frac{1}{2}$ pint (300ml) iced water
$\frac{1}{4}$oz (8g) salt	2 beaten eggs
4oz (100g) lard	4oz (100g) caster sugar
1lb (450g) butter	1 tablespoon lemon juice

Sift the flour and add the salt, then rub in the fat. Use the lard first, and when it has been thoroughly amalgamated with the flour, rub in the butter. This will ensure that the fats are blended and distributed equally throughout the paste. Add a little of the water to the beaten eggs, then toss in the sugar. Add the mixture to the fat/flour dough. Mix gently with a palette knife and then gradually add the lemon juice and the rest of the water, or enough to make a smooth dough. Refrigerate for 1 hour before using.

Pâte à Tartelettes

This paste gives a slightly crisper finish than most other recipes. It is of course ideal for tarts and flans and is used by many establishments in preference to other pastes for such work. It has the great advantage that it may be rolled very thinly without cracking or breaking. The secret of making this paste lies in the proper blending of the fat, sugar and water prior to their being added to the flour.

2lb (900g) plain flour	8oz (225g) caster sugar
¼oz (8g) salt	approximately 1 pint (600ml) cold water
1¼lb (550g) butter	

Sift the flour and salt on to a marble slab (if possible) and make a well in the centre. In a bowl, combine the butter and sugar, mixing thoroughly. When mixed, add most of the water and mix and stir to make a liquid of even consistency. Pour the liquid into the flour and with a fork pull the flour into the well from the sides, mixing gently all the time. When all the flour has been drawn in, clean the fingers and with the heel of the hand smooth out the paste on the slab until it binds together. At this stage you may need to add a little more water, but this will depend upon the type of flour you are using. Fold into a rough rectangle, and leave for 1 hour in a cool place. Then roll into a strip, fold into three and turn the paste around to bring the open edge facing you. Roll out again, fold into three and once more leave for 1 hour before using.

Pâte Frolle

This is a dual-purpose paste, being suitable for a sweet pie crust and as a base for *petit fours*. It is also often used for flans and barquettes when a slightly thicker crust is required.

The procedure for mixing is again slightly different from other pastes, in that the butter is cut into dice and added to the mixture separately.

2lb (900g) plain flour	4 eggs
12oz (325g) caster sugar	1 teaspoon vanilla essence
12oz (325g) ground almonds	1½lb (675g) butter

Sift the flour and tip on to a marble slab or a cool surface, and make a well in the centre. In a bowl, mix the sugar, ground almonds, eggs and essence, then add the butter in small pieces until mixed. Pour into the well of flour, then draw the flour into the liquid as quickly as possible until a paste is formed. Work the paste until smooth, then let it rest for 1 hour before using.

Lining an Unfilled Flan

Line the flan tin in the usual way and prick the base generously with a fork. This will prevent the paste from rising and baking unevenly. Alternatively, place a round of greaseproof paper just large enough to fit snugly in the bottom of the ring, then place a layer of dry haricot beans on the paper. Remove when pastry has set to complete cooking of the base.

Filling a Pie

To prevent the bottom crust becoming soggy when filled with a soft fruit purée, brush the bottom with melted butter.

Glazes

Glazing a two-crust pie gives it an attractive finish, although it does have the effect of toughening the pastry just a little. Here are three fast glazes.

Shiny top Brush the piecrust with milk before baking.

Sugary top Brush first with milk, then sprinkle with caster sugar.

Glazed top Brush with a mixture of whole egg and a little water before baking. This will give a brown, polished finish.

Decorative Edges

A delicious pie deserves an attractive edging. Before you begin to make an edging of any type, fold over the overhanging edge of the dough and mould it into a 'stand-up' rim all around the edge of the tin or plate. Then you may like to try some of the suggestions below.

Braided edge A rather difficult and time-consuming edging for a pie, but most attractive. If you are using this edge for a flan, make enough pastry for a two-crust pie. If you want this edge for a two-crust pie, then an extra piece of pastry will be required. Press the stand-up rim flat, then roll out the remaining pastry and cut into strips about $\frac{1}{4}$in (6mm) wide. You will need a braid measuring approximately 30in (75cm) to edge a 9in (23cm)

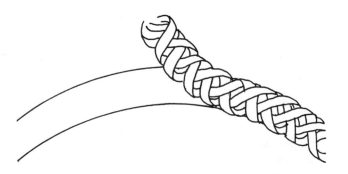

Fig. 150: Placing a braided edge

pie plate. Braid three pieces, brush the rim of the pie plate with water and position the braided edge. Press on to the rim and cut to fit.

Forked edge With a floured 4-tined fork, press the stand-up rim of the pastry down on to the pie or plate at intervals of $\frac{1}{2}$in (1cm). Alternatively, hold the fork at an angle and press a continuous row of 'tine marks' around the pie edge.

Fig. 151: A forked edge

Fluted edge This is one that most people use as a fast finish, although to make a neat and professional edge, practice is necessary. Place the right index finger on the inside of the rim of pastry and the left thumb and index finger on the outside edge. Pinch fingers together, repeating around the edge. Sharpen the points by pinching firmly.

Fig. 152: Making a fluted edge

Polka-dot This is a very simple pattern. Pat the stand-up edge down flat against the rim of the pie plate. Gently press the blunt end of a floured wooden skewer through the pastry on the rim at $\frac{1}{4}$in (6mm) intervals.

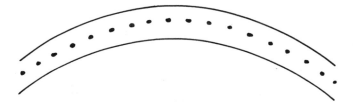

Fig. 153: A polka-dot edge

Rope edge This makes a neat and tailored finish to any pie. Press the stand-up rim with the right thumb held at an angle. Then pinch the pastry between the thumb and knuckle of the index finger at the diagonal.

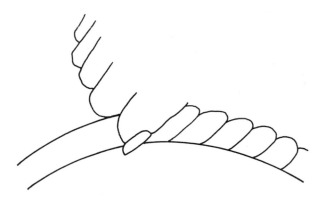

Fig. 154: Making a rope edge

Ruffled edge   This is a variation of the fluted edge. To obtain this effect you place the left thumb and index finger ½in (1cm) apart on the outside of the stand-up rim. With the index finger of the right hand, you *pull* the pastry between the fingers of the left hand, as shown in Fig. 155. Repeat around the entire edge.

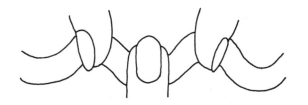

Fig. 155: Making a ruffled edge

Spoon edge   Another very simple decorative design, made by pressing the handle of a teaspoon around the stand-up rim at ¼in (6mm) intervals.

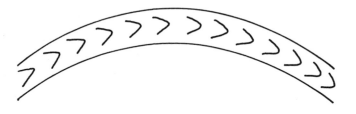

Fig. 156: A spoon edge

Squared edge   Cut small squares from the pastry and then press the stand-up edge down flat against the rim. Overlap the squares of pastry around the edge of the tin.

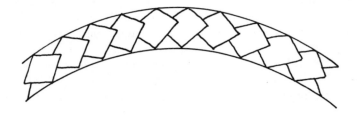

Fig. 157: A squared edge

Puff Pastry Variations

There are a number of different ways in which puff pastry can be prepared to provide something a little different for your guests.

Pinwheel   Roll out the paste to ⅛in (3mm) thickness and cut into 3in (8cm) squares. Using a sharp knife, make four cuts as shown in Fig. 158(a). The incisions are made from each corner to reach to within ¾in (2cm) of the centre. Brush the centre of each square with beaten egg and fold each corner towards the centre. This forms the pinwheel as shown in (b). Press firmly, then brush the surface with eggwash and cook at 350°F (180°C) for about 25 minutes.

When cooked and cold, these pinwheels may be used as an unusually shaped base for a dessert. For example, whipped cream may be piped in the centre and fresh strawberries stuck into the cream. A canned peach-half with a raspberry glaze is another fast but effective idea. A point to remember – to ensure that fruits such as canned peaches, apricots, pine-apple, etc., stay firmly anchored to the pastry, brush a little sugar glaze on to the pastry before placing the fruit in position. Then finish off as required, with a ring of cream around the fruit or a piped rosette of whipped cream with angelica leaves. The centre 'island' left in the pin-wheel gives enough area to position many types of fruit and cream combinations. The same is true of the next design, which is a variation of the pinwheel.

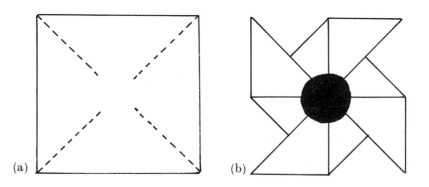

Fig. 158: Puff-pastry pin-wheel. (a): The first cuts; (b): the completed design

(a)   (b)

Maltese cross   The paste is rolled out in the same way as for pinwheels and cut to the same size. Then, with a sharp knife, make cuts as shown in Fig. 159(a). Roll the corner sections towards the centre of the paste, as shown in (b). You may find the 'rolled' sections a little too bulky to provide a neat diamond in the centre of the cross. In this case cut a little of the corner section away before rolling to reduce the bulk. Brush with eggwash before baking. Then use in a similar manner to the pinwheel design.

Palmiers   Although this shape is generally used as an accompaniment to a dessert and served separately, it is an attractive idea to make the palm-iers just a little larger than usual and use them as a base for fruit/whipped

Opposite: Croquembouche decorated with pastry scrolls (page 124–5)

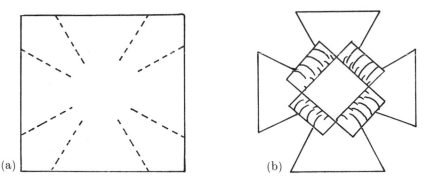

Fig. 159: Maltese cross.
(a): The cuts;
(b): the completed design

(a)   (b)

cream desserts. They are simply made. Roll out the puff paste into an oblong approximately 1×4in ($2 \cdot 5 \times 10$cm), and keep it about $\frac{1}{8}$in (3mm) thick. Brush the surface with beaten egg and arrange each piece on a lightly-floured board, the short side towards you. Fold the paste as shown in Fig. 161, page 122.

After cutting the palmiers, reshape them so that the leaves are evenly spaced. Sprinkle with caster sugar and bake. The chosen dessert (filling) is placed at the end of the palmier, which has a similar shape to that of a scallop shell, and that is the effect it will create when used as suggested.

French Apple Slice

Roll out the puff paste into four lengths about 18×12in (46×30cm). Place two pieces on a baking sheet and spread with apple purée to within 1in ($2 \cdot 5$cm) of the edges. Dampen the edges. Now fold the other two pieces in half lengthways. Cut across the fold at $\frac{1}{4}$in (6mm) intervals leaving 1in ($2 \cdot 5$cm) uncut all along the top and at each end. Open out and lay carefully on top of the purée, sealing the edges firmly. Brush with egg wash and bake in a hot oven for about 25 minutes. Serve cold, sprinkling the surface with icing sugar before cutting into portions.

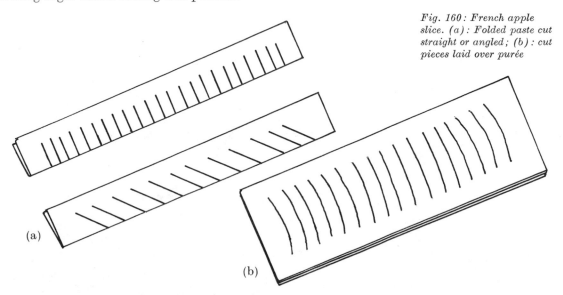

Fig. 160: French apple slice. (a): Folded paste cut straight or angled; (b): cut pieces laid over purée

(a)

(b)

Opposite: Meringue swans on a green jelly lake (126–7)

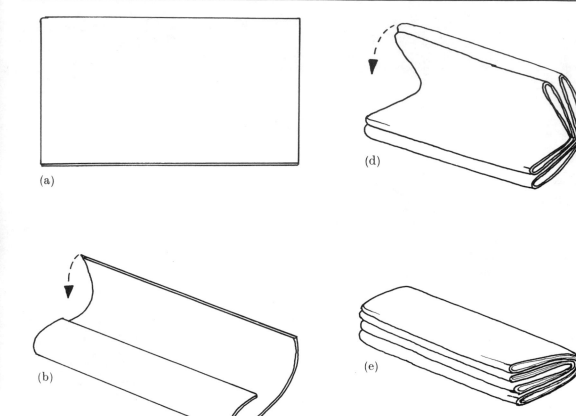

(a)

(b)

(c)

(d)

(e)

(f)

Fig. 161: Palmiers.
(a): Roll to a rectangle
(b): Fold each side into centre
(c): Then fold in half
(d): Fold again the other way
(e): Then cut into $\frac{1}{4}$in (6mm) strips
(f): A palmiers before baking

Fruit Imperial

Roll pastry into an oblong shape about 14×5in (35×13cm). Trim the edges to make a neat shape. Take the remaining pastry and roll into long strips, about ½in (1cm) wide. Transfer the oblong shape on to a damp baking sheet, and brush the edges with water. Lay the strips of pastry along each long side, then knock up and 'flute' the edges with a round-bladed knife. Bake blind. When cooked and cold, take assorted canned fruits and cut them into neat shapes. Soft raw fruits may also be used if desired. Arrange each variety of fruit in lines across the pastry base, then glaze with apricot glaze.

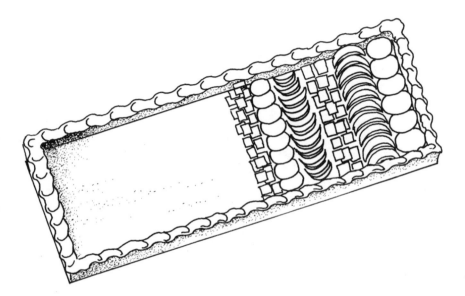

Fig. 162: Fruit Imperial

Apricot glaze   This will give you a full-flavoured glaze suitable for use on most fruits. 6oz (150g) apricot jam, 1 tablespoon brandy, 3 tablespoons water. Heat the jam and water in a saucepan, stirring continually until blended, then add the brandy. Strain through a tammy bag or hair sieve and use while still warm.

Choux Paste

A number of interesting desserts may be produced using choux paste, either baked in the more usual manner or fried (*beignets*). The following is a good recipe.

12oz (325g) flour	10oz (250g) butter
¼oz (8g) salt	1 pint (600ml) egg
1 pint (600ml) water	

Sift the flour and salt on to a strong sheet of paper. Boil the water and butter together in a large saucepan. Remove pan from the heat when the butter is dissolved and stir in the flour quickly. Return to the heat and cook over a low flame for about $\frac{1}{2}$ minute, stirring all the time. Remember that too much cooking for too long or at a too high temperature brings out the fat in the preliminary mixture. The paste should be thoroughly mixed and when ready, will leave the sides of the pan quite easily. Now beat the eggs into the mixture, adding them gradually and beating well between each addition. A check that the proper consistency has been reached is that a little of the dough will stand erect if scooped up on the end of a spoon. The dough is now ready to be made into éclairs, crescents, cream buns, profiteroles or beignets.

Pipe the paste according to the required shape, or, for buns and profiteroles, spoon it on to a baking sheet and bake in a pre-heated oven at 400°F (200°C) for about 35 minutes. Do not touch the shells until they are quite firm, and when taken from the oven be sure that they are not left to cool in a draught. When cool, the shells may be filled with a variety of fillings, confectioner's custard, whipped cream and so on.

Beignets   These are choux paste shapes fried in deep fat – in this manner. Heat the fat to 375°F (190°C). Cut a piece of heavy greaseproof paper to about *half* the size of the fryer. This is to ensure you do not burn your hands. Fill a pastry bag with raw choux paste and, using a star tube, pipe out rings about 2in (5cm) in diameter on the paper. Allow plenty of room between the rings. Take the paper in both hands and tilting it, so that one side is lower than the other, insert it into the fat, keeping the paper side *upwards*. The choux paste rings will drop off into the fat. As they do so, raise the paper on the one side and lower it gradually on the other so that all the rings go into the fat. Allow them to fry for a few minutes until they are an attractive brown on one side, then flip them over to complete the cooking process. Remove from the fat and drain well on absorbent paper. They may be split and filled with custard, cream or jam, or alternatively may be iced with a plain or flavoured icing.

Profiteroles   These small choux paste shells are very versatile in their ability to provide an interesting dessert for the buffet. Here are a few ideas.

Split the cold shells in two and fill one half with whipped cream, then press a fresh strawberry into each and replace the top. Refrigerate until required.

Split the shells, add whipped cream, then crushed pineapple (well drained) and chopped almonds.

Proceed as above, but substitute a flavoured ice-cream for fruit and whipped cream. The ice-cream is scooped from the container with a parisienne cutter. Refrigerate until required.

Croquembouche   This makes a delightful display piece and requires only a little patience to assemble. In the first place it is necessary to caramelise some sugar to act as the means of fixing the profiteroles together.

Heat 12oz (325g) granulated sugar in a heavy saucepan under a very

Fig. 163: Croquembouche

low flame until it is melted and a light straw colour. Then, *very gradually,* add just under ¼ pint (150ml) of boiling water to the syrup. During both of these stages it is essential that the mixture is stirred continuously. Cook for a further 8 minutes or so, still stirring all the time, until the syrup takes on a good golden colour. It is now ready to use.

Pour a little of the syrup to make a thin layer over the dish upon which you intend to build your *croquembouche*. Keep the rest of the syrup warm. Have ready prepared 30 small profiteroles and sufficient whipped cream or confectioner's custard to fill them. Fill the choux cases and then dip the top of each one into the warm syrup. Arrange the profiteroles into a circle about 6in (15cm) in diameter around the rim of the flat service dish, joining them together with the aid of the caramel. Continue to build the choux cases into a pyramid, each layer being formed in decreasing circles.

The pyramid may be additionally decorated by dipping thin leaves of angelica or orange or lemon slices in the warm caramel and attaching them to pastry.

In most of the profiterole ideas mentioned here the choux cases are finished off by being iced with a soft icing, or are served with chocolate sauce.

Polka Tart

This is a combination of short crust and choux paste. Roll out the short crust about ⅛in (3mm) thick and cut a circle approximately 8in (20cm) in diameter. Place the circle on a baking sheet lined with greaseproof paper. Now, using a plain tube, pipe out a rim of choux paste around the edge. Put in the oven and bake at 400°F (200°C) for about 20 minutes or until golden brown. Cool and fill with whipped cream, garnished with fresh fruits.

Turban

On a heavy piece of greaseproof paper, trace a circle about 8in (20cm) in diameter. Using a plain tube, pipe a circular band of choux paste about 1in (2·5cm) thick. Brush with eggwash and sprinkle with raw chopped almonds. Bake in a pre-heated oven at 400°F (200°C) for about 30 minutes, or until the choux paste has dried out. Split the ring horizontally and fill with whipped cream or confectioner's custard. Place the top back in position and dust with icing sugar, or pour chocolate sauce over the ring. Adding a touch of rum and a dash of cinnamon to the chocolate sauce gives it a delightful flavour.

Meringues

These items are a great favourite and are therefore popular as a dessert. Apart from serving them as meringue shells filled with cream, *meringue nests* offer a welcome change when filled with any number of fruit mixtures, with or without whipped cream. Individual nests should be approximately 3in (8cm) in diameter and about 1in (2·5cm) high. *Meringue swans* are one idea not often seen on a buffet. The head and neck is piped out in one piece using a ½in (1cm) plain tube. Using the same tube, the wings are piped in four lines, commencing with the bottom of the wing, each line slightly overlapping the previous one. This gives the finished effect of the wings spreading as they rise from bottom to top.

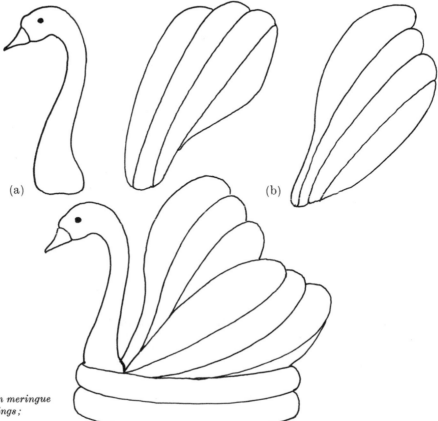

(a)

(b)

Fig. 164: Swan in meringue nest. (a): The wings; (b): the head

For the base of the swan, use a meringue nest, which will give an attract-ive case into which you can put ice-cream or any fruit or cream mixture. After the nest has been filled, fix the head and wings in position with icing or chocolate.

Vacherin Another very popular meringue 'container', this is most useful in a buffet presentation. A vacherin is in effect a meringue case topped with a meringue lid, and is most often made in a size that will serve between 12 and 15 guests – (9in (23cm) in diameter).

The vacherin is made in three parts – the base, the lid and the wall, in this manner. Draw three circles about 9in (23cm) in diameter on a piece of thick greaseproof paper. Using a ½in (1cm) plain tube, fill a piping bag with meringue and, starting from the centre of the circle, pipe the meringue to fill the circle, round and round like a catherine wheel or swiss roll. Repeat on a second circle, so you will have the base and the lid. Pipe around the outer edge of the remaining circle, and build up the sides by piping on top of the first outline to a height of about 1½in (4cm). Strengthen these walls by piping a few criss-cross lines of meringue inside the case. Put the three pieces in a very low oven and leave until quite dry. When ready, fill with the chosen filling. If desired, the meringue may be coloured or three-coloured – white, pink and chocolate. The top of the vacherin need not be just a simple circle design but can be given a flower petal shape, for example.

Fig. 165: Meringue piped tops for vacherin

Flamed Foods

Glamour and a touch of elegance characterises the service of 'flamed foods', and while this type of dessert may not be practical when serving a large number of guests, for the smaller buffet it offers tremendous possibilities. Flaming fruits are of course the simplest form of flambé and are always most effective.

The best 'flame-giver' is brandy, which when flamed burns off the spirit, but the flavour remains. White and dark rum are also good with fruits, as is kirsch. Here are some 'flaming fruit' ideas you may care to try.

Apples

Wash, core and slice but do not peel 4 apples. Heat 4 tablespoons butter in the chafing dish over direct heat. Sauté the apple slices until tender, then sprinkle with 1 tablespoon castor sugar and 4oz (100g) chopped almonds. Pour over 3fl oz apricot brandy that had been previously warmed. Ignite. When flame has died, serve with whipped cream.

Bananas

Bake whole but not too ripe bananas in their skins in a shallow baking dish at 350°F (180°C) for 15 minutes. When cooked, pull away one section of the skin, and ease the fruit away from the remaining skin. Sprinkle the peeled bananas with icing sugar, heat crème de cacao and pour over the bananas.

Cherries

Stone sufficient ripe cherries, then place them in a pan with a light syrup made from 4oz (100g) of sugar dissolved in $\frac{1}{2}$ pint (300ml) water. Poach the fruit until tender, then remove and reduce the syrup to half by fast boiling. Add a touch of cornflour or arrowroot and a pinch of ground ginger to the reduced syrup. Arrange the cherries in an appropriate serving dish and flame them either with brandy or kirsch; serve with vanilla ice-cream.

Mandarins

To each 11oz (300g) can of mandarin oranges, add 2 tablespoons brown sugar and a dash of cinnamon. Place all in a chafing dish or pan with the syrup from the oranges. When the mixture is completely heated through, add 3 tablespoons of brandy and flame. Serve when flame has died.

Peaches

A very elegant dessert! Select whole ripe peaches and peel them carefully. Roll each in sieved raspberry jam. Mix together equal parts of almond chips and sugar and roll the peaches in this mixture until well coated. Arrange in a large, shallow heatproof dish, or silver serving dish. *Do not chill*. Measure a dessertspoon of rum for each peach. Just before serving, put the whole quantity in a metal container. heat thoroughly, allow to ignite, then pour over the peaches. When the flames have died out, serve at once.

Pineapple

Take a whole pineapple and cut 2in (5cm) from the top, leaving the frond in position. Remove the fruit from the shell with a grapefruit knife or a parisienne scoop. Cut this fruit into small pieces and put in a pan with a little sugar (dependent upon the sweetness of the fruit) and 2 tablespoons of brandy. Warm the mixture. Line the pineapple shell with kitchen foil, then pour the fruit back into it. Warm an additional 3 tablespoons of brandy, set it alight and pour over the fruit in the shell. Serve as soon as the flame has died.

Ice-cream with Liqueurs

Turning to ice-cream, some of the simplest but best presentations of this dessert can be achieved by pouring a half measure of liqueur over the ice-cream just before service. Try some of these.

Cherry brandy with vanilla ice-cream.
Kirsch with strawberry.
White Crème de menthe with chocolate or coffee ice-cream.
Crème de cacao for vanilla, chocolate or coffee ice-cream.
Orange curaçao for orange or chocolate ice-cream.
Grand Marnier also for orange or chocolate ice-cream.
Crème de cassis for vanilla or strawberry ice-cream.
Tia Maria for coffee or chocolate ice-cream.

Other fast, simple and effective ice-cream dessert ideas are:

Layer lemon ice-cream, mandarin oranges, chopped almonds and vanilla ice-cream in parfait glasses. Crown with a slice of lemon.
Mix chopped hazelnuts with chopped mixed candied peel, and alternate layers with vanilla ice-cream in parfait glasses. Top with strawberries and sprinkle with chopped nuts.
Place one scoop of lemon ice-cream in centre of a slice of pineapple. Top with a large strawberry and sprinkle with chopped nuts.
Sprinkle a scoop of vanilla ice-cream with chopped hazelnuts. Spoon chocolate sauce over and top with more nuts and a maraschino cherry.
Sprinkle scoops of strawberry ice-cream with toasted hazelnuts. Keep in freezer until ready to serve. Then spoon crushed pineapple over each scoop before serving, garnish with a single strawberry or cherry.

Flaming Ice-cream

This is a simple but spectacular dessert. Combine 4oz (100g) sugar with ¼ pint (150ml) of water and boil for 5 minutes. Remove from the fire and add 2oz (50g) chopped glacé cherries, 2oz (50g) chopped nuts and 4oz (100g) mincemeat. Allow to cool. Put vanilla ice-cream into individual serving dishes and pour the sauce over. Dip a cube of sugar into lemon extract, allowing one cube for each portion, and push slightly into the ice-cream sundae. Ignite the cube and serve flaming.

EMERGENCY DESSERTS

In every section of the kitchen there comes a time when there is an urgent demand for products. Below is a list of 'emergency' desserts – made in a few moments, (providing one stocks a few flan cases and other basics).

Flan Fillings

1 Line a flan case with apple sauce, add a topping of instant whipped cream dusted with a little powered allspice.

2 Line a flan case with fresh strawberries, raspberries or redcurrants. A very quick glaze for these three fruits can be made by warming a jar of cranberry or redcurrant jelly and pouring over the fruit.

3 Line a flan case with mincemeat, cut ring pineapple into wedges. Put one whole ring in centre of flan case and arrange pineapple wedges in lines from outer rim towards centre. Fill hole in pineapple ring with cream or other suitable decoration.

4 Line a flan case with any available fruit. Make a fast topping by whipping together 4 egg whites with 2 tablespoons lemon juice and 2 tablespoons caster sugar. When peaked, spread over fruit and sprinkle with chopped nuts. (*Note:* 4 egg-white recipe will cover 3 × 9in (23cm) flans.)

5 Fold drained, canned fruit cocktail into whipped cream or instant topping slightly flavoured with almond essence. Pile into flan cases and garnish with chocolate curls.

6 Fill a pre-cooked flan case with vanilla ice-cream soft enough to spread. Sprinkle with chopped glacé fruits. Place whole fresh strawberries or raspberries on top. Finish off with a whipped cream decoration. Refrigerate until needed.

Pots de Crème Mocha

To 1 package of instant chocolate pudding (there are a number of brands) add 1 teaspoon of instant coffee and then make up to manufacturer's directions, but use half milk, half single cream instead of all milk, and add 1 beaten egg. Pour into one large or more individual moulds and decorate with chocolate curls.

Chocolate curls Allow a slab of semi-sweet chocolate to stand in its wrapper in a warm place for about 15 minutes to soften. To make large curls, unwrap the slab and carefully draw a vegetable parer or potato peeler across the wider surface of the block of chocolate. For small curls, draw the parer across the side of the block. Lift the curls with a cocktail stick to prevent breaking. Put in refrigerator to allow them to stiffen.

Index

Abstract design 26
    motifs 22
Alsace salad 72
Aluminium moulds 31
Anchovy 39–40
Appetisers 61
    on sticks 62–4
Apples flambé 128
Apple corer 47
Apple slice, French 121
Application of design to form 18
Argenteuil salad 72
Apricot glaze 123
Artichoke 40
    Globe 63
Asparagus 40–1
Aspic cutters 31–3
    jelly 58, 98
    painting 59–60
Astoria salad 72
Aubergine 58, 63
Avocado 67

Bags, Piping 31
Balance 18–20
Bananas flambé 128
Barquettes 65
Baskets, Cucumber 46
    Lemon 48–50
    Melon 50

Potato 64–4
Tomato 55
Beans, Green 48
Beef 106
    consommé 84
Beetroot 41
Beignets 124
Blades, Metal for knife 29
Boats, Caviar 65–6
    Crab and tomato 66
    Cucumber 46
    Devilled ham 66
    Sardine and cheese 66
    Tuna 66
Border patterns 11
Bouchées 66
'Breaks' 43
Brilat salad 72
Broccoli 41–2
Butter curler 31
Butter, Savoury 87–8
Butterfly, Lemon 48

Caisses 66–7
Canapés 94–9
    Emergency 98–9
    'Royal' 96–8
    Standard 95–6
Capers 43
Carolines 66
Carrot 43–4

Cauliflower 42
Caviar 42–3
Celery 44
Chain, Cucumber 46
Cherries flambé 128
Chicken 113
   consommé 84
Chives 45
Chocolate curls 130
Choux paste 123–6
Circular panels 22
Colour 27
   combinations 27
   contrast 8
Companions, Soup 85
Consommé, Beef 84
   Chicken 84
Containers, Bread 66–7
   Dip 62
   Meringue 127
   Pastry 65–6
   Sauce 53
Corn, Sweet 43, 45
Cornets 66
Cornucopias, Sandwich 91
Correspondence of contour 12
   of line 12
Counter-balance 19, 20
Crab 104
Crawfish 105
Crayfish 104–5
Cream soups 84
Creole salad 73
Croquembouche 124–5
Croûtons 85
Crown roast of lamb 107
Cucumber 45–7
Curls, Carrot 44
   Celery 44
   Chocolate 130
   Cucumber 46
   Lemon 48
Curve declensions 12, 24
   of force 13–14
Cutters, Aspic 31
   Metal 31
   Parisienne 31
Cut-out designs 57, 58–9
Cutlets 108–9

Decorative platters 22
   salads 75–6
Design formulation 20–1
Desserts, Emergency 130
Diamond panels 22
Dips 61–2
Draughtboard sandwiches 90
Dressing, French 82
   Salad 82–3
DuBarry salad 73
Duchesse salad 73

Edges for flans, Decorative 117–19
Eggs 47–8
   Stuffed 69–71
Eggslice 31
Emergency canapés 98–9
   desserts 130
Envelopes, Sandwich 91

Fan, Gherkin 48
   Radish 54
Fern, Cucumber 46
Fish 101–6
Flamed foods 127–9
Flans 117–19
   fillings, Emergency 130
Flavourmates, Soup 84–5
Flemish salad 73
Floats, Soup 86
Flowers, Beetroot 41
   Carrot 43
   Pimento 54
   Radish 54
   Smoked salmon 71
   Tomato 55
   Turnip 56
Flower and leaf designs 17, 20, 21, 22
Focal point 18
Fonds d'artichauts farcis 40
Formal balance 19
Freehand design 57–9

French apple slice 122
   dressing 82
Frosting grapes 68
Fruit Imperial 123
Fruit salad 50
   Easily moulded 81–2

Gala salad 73
Garlic bread 85
Gateau, Sandwich 92
Gelatine for moulded salads 76
   substitute for truffles 57
Gherkins 48
Glaze, Apricot 123
   for flans 117
Globe artichoke 63
Golden rectangle 15
Grapefruit 68
Grapes, Frosting 68
Grinds of knife blades 30
Gros piéces 40

Half-circular panels 21–2
Ham 40, 110–11
Horse and chariot effect 104–5
Horseradish cream 71

Ice-cream, Flaming 129
   with Liqueurs 129
Impressions 24
Inceptive axis 19, 20, 22
Informal balance 19, 20
Internal structure 24
Italian salad 73

Jelly, Aspic 58, 98

Knives 24–31

Lamb 107–9
   Crown roast of 107
   Saddle of 108
   Cutlets 108–9
Leek 48
Lemon 48–50
Line 9, 10–14
Links, Unifying 11–12
Lobster 103–4
   Bellevue 104
   Parisienne 103–4
Lumpfish roe 42–3

Mass 9, 14–20
Maltese cross pastries 120
Mandarines flambé 128
Mandolin 31
Mayonnaise 83
Meat 106–11
Medallions of salmon 102–3
Melba toast 85
Melon 50–1, 68–9
Meringues 126–7
Metals for knife blades 29
Mosaic sandwiches 90–1
Moulded salads 76–82
   Fruit 81–2
   Garnishing 81
   Liquors for 79, 80
   Making 79
   Unmoulding 80–1
Moulds, Aluminium 31
Mushroom 51

Nests, Meringue 126

Olive tree 52
Olives 51–3
Onion 41
Onward movement 11
Open sandwiches 93
Optical rhythms 9
Outlines 24
Outline design 57–8
Oval panels 22

Painting, Aspic 59–60
Palais Royal salad 73
Palmiers 120–1, 122
Panels, Circular 22
    Diamond 22
    Half-circular 21–2
    Oval 22
    Square 22
    Triangular 21–2
Parisienne cutters 31, 50, 67, 126
Parsley 48, 53
    tree 64
Pastry brushes 31
Pâté 47
Pâte à Foncée 115–16
    à Tartélettes 116
    Frolle 116
Patricia salad 73–4
Patty pans 31
Peaches flambé 128
Peas 43
Peppers 41, 53
Pimento 40, 47, 53, 54
Pin cushion (display) 62
Pineapple flambé 128–9
    juice in moulded salads, Warning about 79
Pinwheel sandwiches 88
Pinwheels (pastries) 120

Piping bags and tubes 31
Platter of meat 26
    salads, Designs for 73, 74, 77, 78
Polka tart 125
Pork 110
Potato baskets 64–5
Pots de crème mocha 130
Poultry 112–13
Prawns 105–6
Presentation 8
Principles of design 9
Profiteroles 124
Proportion 15–18
    division 17

Radiation 14, 22
Radish 42, 54
Razor blade 58
Representational design 23–6
Restful designs 11
Restraint 7
Reversing the shape 25
Rhythm 15
Rib of beef, Standing 40, 106
Ribbon sandwiches 88–9
Rings, Melon 68
'Royal' canapés 96–8

Saddle of lamb 108
Salads 22
    Combination 72–4
    Fruit 50
    Decorative 75–6
    Moulded 76–82
Salad bowls 26
    dressings 82–3
Salmon, 101–2
    Medallions of 102–3
    Smoked 71–2
Sandwiches 87–94
    Gateau 92
    Open 93–4

Savouries, Bacon-wrapped 64
Saw-toothed knife blade 31
Scalloped knife blade 31
Scorers, Vegetable 31
Scroll links 11–12
Serrated-edge knife blade 31
Shears, Kitchen 29
Shellfish 67, 103–6
Shrimp tree 53
Shrimps 106
Skewers, Decorative 47
Smoked salmon 71–2
  trout 71
Soup 83–5
  companions 85
  floats 86
Spatula 31
Special shapes, Designing of 20–3
Square panels 22
Star shapes 16
Static form 22–3
Strainers 65
Stuffed eggs 69–71
  olives 51
Suckling pig, Roast 110
Summation series 16
Swans 126
Symmetry 14–15

Tang of knife 30, 31
Tart, Polka 125
Tartlette 41, 66
Testing knives 30
Toast floats 85
  Melba 85
Tomato 55

Tongue 56
Treatment of verticals 21
Tree designs 25, 26
  Olive 52
  Parsley 64
  Shrimp 53
Triangular panels 21–2
Trout, Smoked 71
Truffles 56–7
Tubes, Piping 31
Turban 125–6
Turkey 113
Turnip 56
Turnovers, Pastry 64
Turtle soup, Clear 84
Tweezers 31, 58, 59
Twists, Cucumber 45
Types of design 23–6

Unit technique 24–5
Unity 18

Vacherin 127
Variety 18
Vegetable scorers 31

Watercress 57, 68
Wedges, Lemon 48